HOBSBAWM

HOBSBAWM

History and Politics

GREGORY ELLIOTT

PlutoPress
www.plutobooks.com

First published 2010 by Pluto Press
345 Archway Road, London N6 5AA and
175 Fifth Avenue, New York, NY 10010

www.plutobooks.com

Distributed in the United States of America exclusively by
Palgrave Macmillan, a division of St. Martin's Press LLC,
175 Fifth Avenue, New York, NY 10010

British Library Cataloguing in Publication Data
A catalogue record for this book is available from the British Library

ISBN   978 0 7453 2845 4   Hardback
ISBN   978 0 7453 2844 7   Paperback

Library of Congress Cataloging in Publication Data applied for

This book is printed on paper suitable for recycling and made from fully
managed and sustained forest sources. Logging, pulping and manufacturing
processes are expected to conform to the environmental standards of the
country of origin.

10   9   8   7   6   5   4   3   2   1

Designed and produced for Pluto Press by
Chase Publishing Services Ltd, 33 Livonia Road, Sidmouth, EX10 9JB, England
Typeset from disk by Stanford DTP Services, Northampton, England
Printed and bound in the European Union by
CPI Antony Rowe, Chippenham and Eastbourne

For Emmanuel and Natasha

CONTENTS

ABBREVIATIONS

CPGB   Communist Party of Great Britain
CPSU   Communist Party of the Soviet Union
CPUSA Communist Party of the United States of America
HSWP   Hungarian Socialist Workers' Party
PCE   Spanish Communist Party
PCF   French Communist Party
PCI   Italian Communist Party
UP   Unidad Popular / Socialist Party of Chile

PREFACE

In one sense – one only – Eric Hobsbawm is last among equals. At the time of writing, he is virtually the sole surviving member of the remarkable group of Marxist historians – Christopher Hill and V. G. Kiernan, Rodney Hilton and George Rudé, John Saville and E. P. Thompson – formed in the British Communist Party from the mid 1930s; and it has been his sad duty, as well as privilege, to record the passing of these and other colleagues over the last two decades.[1]

In his obituary of Thompson in 1993, Hobsbawm generously observed:

> He was the only historian I knew who had not just talent, brilliance, erudition and the gift of writing, but the capacity to produce something qualitatively different from the rest of us, not to be measured on the same scale. Let us simply call it genius, in the traditional sense of the word. ... The loss to intellectual life, history and the British Left cannot yet be calculated.[2]

Unlike Thompson, Hobsbawm has not been taken from us prematurely. In the 16 years he has outlived his friend, he has consolidated a cumulative contribution to intellectual life, history and the left well beyond Britain which, if less immediately outstanding than Thompson's, will prove equally enduring. Not a great writer – albeit a very fine one – and a Marxist of a very different temperament, if no single book by Hobsbawm has the *éclat* of *The Making of the English Working Class*, it is likely that *Age of Extremes* is the one text, aside from the classics, that any educated Marxist anywhere will – certainly should – have read.

Since the appearance of Hobsbawm's history of the 'short twentieth century' in 1994, and its more or less rapid translation into dozens of languages, it has become commonplace for its author to find himself characterised as one of the world's most famous living historians, if not quite simply the most famous. Since then, he has made the transition from the status of academic historian to 'public intellectual' (not to be confused with TV don); and as such is regularly invited to employ his professional authority to pronounce on the issues of the day. His name and work are as familiar in Italy or Brazil, the USA or India, as they are in the UK. If age has wearied him as he approaches his 93rd birthday, neither his productivity nor his topicality shows any obvious sign of flagging, with *Globalisation, Democracy and Terrorism* released in March 2007, regular articles published in the *London Review of Books* and elsewhere thereafter, and a collection on Marx and Marxism promised for January 2011.

In the course of a career stretching back to the 1940s, Hobsbawm has become an inescapable reference-point in an extraordinary variety of subjects that cut across national and disciplinary boundaries. The best known of these is doubtless his survey of the making of modernity in the 'Ages' tetralogy. But he has also been a major protagonist, for example, in debates over the transition to capitalism in Europe; working classes and labour movements, peasants and bandits; the vicissitudes of communism and nationalism; receptions of the French Revolution and questions of historiography.

Given his fertility and celebrity, the relative dearth of in-depth writing on Hobsbawm is striking. There are, of course, countless reviews of individual texts, some of them incisive. To date, however, no more than a single short book in Spanish – an undemanding primer – appears to have been devoted to him.[3] In English perhaps only Harvey Kaye's now dated chapter in his *British Marxist Historians*, and an authoritative two-part review article by Perry Anderson, have begun to range over anything like Hobsbawm's oeuvre as a whole.[4]

One day, an attempt will have to be made to take the cue provided by Hobsbawm's autobiography, *Interesting Times*, and venture a full-scale historical and critical study. Here, meanwhile, something much more modest has been prompted by the fact that the *pro forma* plaudits of recent years, downplaying Hobsbawm's Marxism and communism, have begun to be countered by voices from the centre and right. These go to prove the justice of Hobsbawm's claim that, as someone who remained in the Communist Party until its dissolution in 1991, and who has 'systematically refused to abjure his past', he possesses 'not only the interest of scarcity but of incomprehensibility'.[5] Thus, *Interesting Times* attracted several highly critical reviews (and at least one hysterical rant) on account of that refusal.[6] *Globalisation, Democracy and Terrorism* was taken to task for its criticism of capitalism and deflation of the holy of holies, liberal democracy.[7] And in 2009 Hobsbawm's application to see the file held on him by MI5 afforded an opportunity for populist fulminations in the *Daily Mail* impressive for their iniquity and inanity alike.[8]

Hobsbawm: History and Politics endeavours to capture something of its subject's 'scarcity' and 'incomprehensibility', rendering him more comprehensible but no less scarce for that. Unusual, if not unique, among his comrades in publishing memoirs, Hobsbawm's were written from the left, but not (unlike Saville's) for it.[9] Adjusting the balance, Chapter 1 explores the making of a communist militant and Marxist historian from 1917–56, complementing and (where necessary) qualifying Hobsbawm's own depiction of 'a twentieth-century life'. Chapter 2 turns to three key topics in the work of the mature historian – his 'progressivist' conception of history, his observation of international developments in Marxism and communism post-1956, and his participation in debates over the British labour movement. A third chapter, which elaborates at length on a previous short text,[10] undertakes a detailed examination of Hobsbawm's account of the twentieth century and its immediate aftermath, in the light of the preceding trilogy on the 'long nineteenth century'.

Much has been reluctantly omitted from this brief profile – most obviously, investigation of Hobsbawm's writings on nationalism and his interventions on historiography, which belie his sometime self-description as 'a sufficiently British historian to wish to concentrate on brass tacks, namely, what happened and why'.[11] (Readers interested in trends in history as an academic discipline since the 1960s can do no better than turn to Geoff Eley's consistently illuminating *A Crooked Line*.[12]) The present book will have served a purpose if it provokes others to remedy its omissions and misinterpretations, and provides some pointers for the intellectual biography which, if anyone does, Eric Hobsbawm surely warrants.

Hobsbawm once wrote that 'the historian's business is not praise and blame, but analysis'.[13] It is a self-denying ordinance its author has honoured as much in the breach as the observance, and for the better – crisp parenthetical judgements being one of his invariably pleasurable trademarks. As a work of intellectual history, *Hobsbawm: History and Politics*, whose title is intended as a passing tribute to Louis Althusser's little gem of a book on Montesquieu, prioritises synthesis and analysis. But it does not abstain from evaluation, the overall tenor of which will soon become evident to readers to whose judgement these pages must now in turn be submitted.

ACKNOWLEDGEMENTS

I am grateful to Anne Beech and her colleagues at Pluto Press for their patience and encouragement; to Geoff Eley, Keith McLelland and an anonymous referee for their constructive reports; and to Keith McLelland again for allowing me sight of his as yet unpublished, up-to-date bibliography of Hobsbawm's writings. Once more, my family generously allowed me the time, and my neighbour Ian Horobin the space, to write.

Gregory Elliott
Edinburgh, 10 December 2009

1
FORMATIVE EXPERIENCES, REFOUNDING MOMENTS

A man lives not only his personal life, as an individual, but also, consciously or unconsciously, the life of his epoch and his contemporaries.

Thomas Mann, *The Magic Mountain*

'Little bits of all the world were to be found in Eric', observed a Cambridge contemporary, subsequently general secretary of the Ceylonese Communist Party, in 1939.[1] At all events, much of Europe – and more besides – contributed to the making of E. J. Hobsbawm.

He was born in Alexandria, in June 1917, to Jewish parents – an anglophile Austrian mother, one of three daughters of a Viennese jeweller, and a British father, one of eight children of a London cabinet-maker. Once the First World War had ended, the family moved to Vienna, capital of a federation created out of the debris of the Habsburg Empire. '[N]ot only a state which did not want to exist, but a predicament which could not last',[2] the first Austrian republic did not survive for long, political polarisation between Catholic reactionaries and reformist socialists exploding into civil war in 1934, with the winning clerical side ceding to a feted *Anschluss* four years later. Meanwhile, for the duration of Hobsbawm's residence, if English parentage on the paternal side afforded a measure of protection against the city's notorious anti-Semitism, the conventional middle-class lifestyle of non-observant, assimilated Jewry turned out to be unsustainable amid the great post-war inflation. His father, 'spectacularly unsuited for the jungle of the market economy', died in 1929, at the age of 48, leaving the family 'temporarily destitute'.[3] A mother who declined to dispense with the services of a maid she could ill afford, followed her husband to the grave two-and-a-half years later, aged 36. The sacrifice involved in the purchase of an atlas needed for geography classes at his *Gymnasium*; recourse to a Jewish charity for an indispensable new pair of shoes; acute embarrassment over the reconditioned second-hand bike given as a birthday present – such childhood memories convey something of the constant insecurity, bordering on poverty, that marked these years. The bike was disposed of as soon as was decently possible; the *Kozenn-Atlas*, like his mother's copy of Karl Kraus's *The Last Days of Humanity*, has been preserved. As has another maternal bequest, consisting in a 'simple principle': 'never do anything, or seem to do anything that might suggest that you are ashamed of being a Jew'.[4]

Decisive Years

Following his mother's death in July 1931, Hobsbawm transferred to Berlin to live with his aunt and uncle, who had found a job there with Universal Films (the Hollywood studio that had made Remarque's *All Quiet on the Western Front* the previous year). This was 'the city in which I spent the two most decisive years of my life'.[5] 'It is difficult', Hobsbawm writes,

> for those who have not experienced the 'Age of Catastrophe' of the twentieth century in central Europe to see what it meant to live in a world that was simply not expected to last, in something that could not really even be described as a world, but merely as a way-station between a dead past and a future not yet born, unless perhaps in the depths of revolutionary Russia. Nowhere was this more palpable than in the dying days of the Weimar Republic.[6]

By then, the respite from the mass misery and despair of 1918–23 provided by the stabilisation of the mid 1920s had evaporated. The collapse of the world economy at the close of the decade, devastating workers and demoralising the middle classes, had electrified politics in a country where resentment of the punitive provisions imposed by the Entente at Versailles was well-nigh universal. In the burgeoning ranks of the ascendant far right, a revanchist nationalism super-charged by anti-Semitism targeted 'Judeo-Bolshevism' as the proximate cause of Germany's woes – and its eradication, at home and abroad, as the precondition of imperial regeneration. After fourteen inglorious years that belied its cultural splendours – the *Kulturbolschewismus* detested by National Socialism – Weimar, whose legitimacy had never been accepted by the right, and which was rejected with equal vehemence by the far left as 'a restoration of economic, social, political and legal injustice'[7] – the Reich without the Hohenzollerns – would fall victim to counter-revolution.

'What could young Jewish intellectuals have become under such circumstances?', Hobsbawm mused four decades later:

> Not liberals of any kind, since the world of liberalism (which included social democracy) was precisely what had collapsed. As Jews we were precluded by definition from supporting parties based on confessional allegiance, or on a nationalism which excluded Jews, and in both cases on anti-semitism. We became either communists or some equivalent form of revolutionary marxists, or if we chose our own versions of blood-and-soil nationalism, Zionists. But even the great bulk of young intellectual Zionists saw themselves as some sort of revolutionary marxist nationalists. There was virtually no other choice. We did not make a commitment against bourgeois society and capitalism, since it patently seemed to be on its last legs. We simply chose a future rather than *no* future, which meant revolution. The great October revolution and Soviet Russia proved that such a new world was possible, perhaps that it was already functioning.[8]

The choice, so it seemed at the apocalyptic time, was 'between ruin and revolution – for Left or Right – between no future and a future'.[9] German social-democracy, more nearly resembling Jaroslav Hasek's 'Party of Moderate and Peaceful Progress Within the Limits of the Law' than its Austrian counterpart, manifestly failed to fit the bill.

Discovery of *The Communist Manifesto* in the library of the Prinz-Heinrichs *Gymnasium* attended by

Hobsbawm imparted some intellectual underpinning to political conviction. Translation of theory into practice came with his recruitment into a communist secondary-school students' organisation, the Sozialistischer Schulerbund (SSB), in the autumn of 1932. Hobsbawm recalls 'no signs of discouragement' in his cell in West Berlin, as it shouldered the task of helping to halt Hitler's rise to power. What he realises to have been the 'suicidal idiocy' of its parent organisation's ultrasectarian line of 1928–33 – the 'class against class' dictated by the Comintern but eagerly embraced by the German Communist Party (KPD) – had it that social-democracy alone stood between the working class and its revolutionary radicalisation. Hence – fatal conceit of the 'Third Period' – even were a perfect storm on the streets to be blowing from the right, and the Nazis to prevail courtesy of 'social fascism', their triumph would prove fleeting, followed in short order by a proletarian revolution led by the KPD, with its hundreds of thousands of members and millions of voters.[10] 'After Hitler, our turn', as the slogan had it – not so much socialism *or* barbarism as barbarism *then* socialism. The upshot? A fast-motion disaster. As Hobsbawm wrote in 1970, in a verdict that may be extended to the uncomprehending teenage militant, the KPD 'did not even realise that it was failing, until long after it was too late, let alone how catastrophically and irrevocably it had failed. And so it went down to a total and final defeat.'[11]

Sceptical of the notion that an anti-fascist united front, assuming the Social Democratic Party (SPD) had consented to it, could have averted the calamity,[12] Hobsbawm rejects the *canard* of communist complicity in Nazi triumph. Three arresting snapshots round off his memories of Weimar. The first is a depiction of the KPD's last legal demonstration, exuding vain defiance, on a perishing winter's day on 25 January 1933. The second is an evocation of the moment five days later, when he read the headline announcing Hindenburg's appointment of Hitler as Chancellor – something 'I can see ... still, as in a dream'.[13] ('Moments when one knows history has changed are rare, but this was one of them', Hobsbawm has recently remarked.)[14] The last, prefaced as the historian's 'introduction to a characteristic experience of the communist movement: doing something hopeless and dangerous because the Party told us to',[15] is campaigning for the KPD in the March elections and sheltering the SSB's duplicator after the Reichstag fire had rendered an already bad situation impossible.

Of course, Hobsbawm was among the fortunate ones, emigrating with his sister to London just as Hitler unveiled a boycott of Jewish businesses in early April 1933. 'After the excitement of Berlin, Britain was inevitably a comedown.'[16] Addressing survivors of his old London school at their annual reunion in 2007, he invited them to

> Imagine yourselves as a newspaper correspondent based in Manhattan and transferred by your editor to Omaha, Nebraska. That's how I felt when I came to England after almost two years in the most unbelievably exciting, sophisticated, intellectually and politically explosive Berlin of the Weimar Republic. The place was a terrible letdown.[17]

And yet, immigrant but not foreigner, the blue-eyed, fair-haired boy whom his Berlin schoolmates had referred to as 'Der Englander' (rather than 'Der Jude') would appear by the end of the decade to have acquired what Pieter Keunemann affectionately portrayed as 'a large and vulgar patriotism for England, which he considered in weak moments as his spiritual home'.[18]

By contrast with the crises convulsing the continent, the United Kingdom, for all the regionally uneven impact of the slump, was experiencing something of an imperial Indian summer. Forced off the gold standard and out of free trade, it could shelter in the empire artificially inflated by the victors in 1919. Politically, the comparative torpor of the country, ruled since 1931 by a National Government that obtained a 'doctor's mandate' four years later (and would probably have won the election scheduled for 1940), was not compensated for by any experience of adolescent activism. Banned by his adoptive parents from joining the (mass but reformist) Labour Party, let alone the (revolutionary but miniscule) Communist Party, Hobsbawm pretty much 'lived a life of suspended political animation' until he went up to Cambridge in

1936.[19] Culturally, too, London could scarcely compete with Berlin, where he had encountered the fiction of Mann and Döblin, the poetry as well as the dramaturgy of Brecht, the music of Weil. Educationally, however, it meant St Marylebone Grammar School, where he was 'introduced ... to the astonishing marvels of English poetry and prose' and 'took to examinations as to ice-cream'.[20] With astonishing rapidity, Hobsbawm's grammar school equipped him to win a scholarship to Cambridge University, with the choice of reading for a degree in three or more subjects, launching him on a brilliant *cursus* (tarnished, if at all, only by the original option for King's over Balliol). Voracious reading – concomitant of an 'ultra-intellectualisation' that can be regarded as a sublimation of political, not to mention other, more familiar adolescent passions – was counter-pointed by one genuinely exciting and enduring artistic revelation, on a par with anything vouchsafed by Weimar: jazz. Inducted into it by a cousin, Hobsbawm enthusiastically greeted 'the dimension of wordless, unquestioning physical emotion into a life otherwise almost monopolized by words and the exercises of the intellect'.[21]

The undergraduate is said to have 'admit[ted] a love of literature, English, French and German, but only specifies Thurber. Otherwise sticks to Lenin and Stalin.'[22] The autobiographer is similarly reticent about his reading – frustratingly so. As to what he made of it, and it of him,

The short answer is: I tried to give it a Marxist, that is to say an essentially historical, interpretation. There was not much else to do for an impassioned but unorganised and necessarily inactive communist teenage intellectual. Since I had not read much more than the *Communist Manifesto* when I left Berlin ... I ... had to acquire some knowledge of Marxism. My Marxism was, and still to some extent remains, that acquired from the only texts then easily available outside university libraries, the systematically distributed works and selections of 'the classics' published ... under the auspices of the Marx-Engels Institute in Moscow.[23]

In other words, as he proceeds to note, Hobsbawm's Marxism was – though it scarcely remained – the authorised version of Marxism-Leninism standardised, under Stalin's signature, in the section on 'Dialectical and Historical Materialism' from the 1938 *Short Course* on the history of the CPSU:

It corresponded pretty much to what I, and perhaps most of the British intellectual reds of the 1930s, understood by Marxism. We liked to think of it as 'scientific' in a rather nineteenth-century sense. ... What made Marxism so irresistible was its comprehensiveness. 'Dialectical materialism' provided, if not a 'theory of everything', then at least a 'framework [for] everything', linking inorganic and organic nature with human affairs, collective and individual, and providing a guide to the nature of all interactions in a world in constant flux.[24]

Like several British Marxist historians – Hill, Kiernan and Thompson are among those cited – Hobsbawm graduated to historiography 'from, or with, a passion for *literature*', the subject which, in the English secondary-school curriculum, did duty for the philosophy taught at continental *lycées* and *Gymnasia*. (Hence the impact of Leavis on Hobsbawm and so many others who scarcely shared his politics.) His Marxism, he tells us, developed as an endeavour to understand the relationship between art and society through the optic of the classical Marxist base/superstructure topography, rather than the overall trajectory of human history projected by Marx's 1859 Preface and bowdlerised by the Stalinist rendition of historical materialism.

An unflattering self-portrait drawn in his diary at the start of 1936 gives us a unique glimpse of the schoolboy's sense of self:

> Eric John Ernest Hobsba[w]m, a tall, angular, dangly, ugly, fair-haired fellow of eighteen and a half, quick on the uptake, with a considerable if superficial stock of general knowledge and a lot of original ideas, general and theoretical. An incorrigible striker of attitudes, which is all the more dangerous and at times effective, as he talks himself into believing in them himself. Not in love and apparently quite successful at sublimating his passions, which – not often – find expression in the ecstatic enjoyment of nature and art. Has no sense of morality, thoroughly selfish. Some people find him extremely disagreeable, others likeable, yet others (the majority) just ridiculous. He wants to be a revolutionary but, so far, shows no talent for organization. He wants to be a writer, but without energy and the ability to shape the material. He hasn't got the faith that will move the necessary mountains, only hope. He is vain and conceited. He is a coward. He loves nature deeply. And he forgets the German language.[25]

The prose, sardonic and laconic, contains more than a hint of the adult writer, suggesting something other than an essay in ingratiating self-depreciation – the familiar syndrome of *qui s'accuse s'excuse*. But if this was 'the spirit [in which] I faced the year 1936 and Cambridge University', it is the last exercise in introspection undertaken by the autobiographer. With the move to Cambridge, a transition occurs in *Interesting Times* to a version of the more collective, generational reportage and reflection exemplified by his fellow Kingsman and friend, Noel Annan, in – the title says it all – *Our Age*.

Dynamique unitaire?

As it happens, a few lines from that book are possibly more informative about, or at any rate evocative of, the student Hobsbawm than the bulk of his own chapters[26] – certainly more so than the 'intermezzo' on the Cambridge spies with which he opens his account of the university and communism. It is not that Hobsbawm disavows Burgess et al. ('most of us – certainly I – would have taken [such work] on ourselves, if asked').[27] Rather, the 'lines of loyalty [which] ran not between but across countries' – and not only in the 1930s but thereafter, and not solely *between* political families but *within* them – are drawn here with a dispassionate detachment that does less than justice to the complexity and intensity of the subject.[28]

Of course, this might be regarded as a perfectly legitimate ground-clearing operation, conducted in the warranted belief that (as Hobsbawm put it during the hunt for the 'Fourth Man' in 1979) 'searching for spies is not ... the best way to understand the 1930s'.[29] How, then, does *Interesting Times* contribute to an understanding of Hobsbawm's 1930s? Aside from the intellectual excitement of lectures on economic history by the medievalist M. M. Postan, who introduced undergraduates to Marc Bloch and *Annales*, Hobsbawm seems to have derived little stimulus from his teachers on the History Tripos, 'not an intellectually very demanding subject' in the comprehensively archaic Cambridge of the time.[30] But if he stopped frequenting the lecture theatre, quit the Cambridge Union and gave up learning Russian – a choice 'which has confined me to remaining a purely western cosmopolitan'[31] – this left all the more time for Hobsbawm's central student experience: politics.

He at once joined the student branch of the Communist Party (CP), ending up on its three-person secretariat ('the highest political function I have ever occupied'), and the Cambridge University Socialist Club. Giving the lie to the myth of 'Red Cambridge', Hobsbawm writes that at its peak in early 1939 the latter counted 1,000 members – still something over 20 per cent of the undergraduate body – while the former never mustered much over 100 card-carriers. Of his own individual activities directly in or deriving from the CP, in truth, *Interesting Times* divulges little of interest. We learn that he spent summer holidays in Paris – now the Comintern's European centre – to work with an inscrutable James Klugmann ('[h]e gave nothing away'),[32] who had moved from leadership of the CP at Cambridge to head up a student front organisation there. (Thus, Hobsbawm acted as translator at its 1937 congress, coinciding with the World Exposition at which Soviet and Nazi pavilions glowered at each other across the Champ de Mars.) Also alluded to in this context is Margot Heinemann, former partner of Klugmann's co-leader of Cambridge communists, John Cornford, killed in Spain in 1936. Of her, no more – and no less – is said than that 'she probably had more influence on me than any other person I have known'.[33] Otherwise, the chapters notionally devoted to this phase of *his* life – 'Cambridge' and 'Against Fascism and War' – are for the most part generically concerned with the 'Cambridge reds'.

Faced with the serial crises and emergencies of the 1930s, they 'campaigned: constantly, passionately, and in a spirit of hopeful confidence that surprises me as I look back'.[34] Far from being the 'low dishonest decade' of Auden's revisionist retrospect, for them the 1930s were 'a time when the good cause confronted its enemies'[35] – as it still did in 1952 when, against the background clamour of conversions to the right, Hobsbawm wrote as an 'unregenerate survivor' of the 1930s in defence of them:

> those who do not feel in their bones what we learned in Cambridge fifteen years ago, the desire to build a good society, and the confidence that it can be done, will not understand what all the

noise is about. We the unregenerate survivors of the 'Thirties are not therefore trying to get 1952 to imitate us. ... We merely wish to state that ... we still don't feel homesick for any other Cambridge generation ... or anybody else's lifetime except ours. Thank you, we are quite happy as we are.[36]

Of the three reasons given by Hobsbawm for comparative good cheer at the time, two – the fact that the left had a single enemy (fascism plus its active or passive collaborators) and had taken up arms against it in Spain – might with equal plausibility have given cause for concern, since the enemy had not ceased to be victorious, with Spain about to fall to it next. The third – 'we thought we knew what the new world would be like after the old world had come to an end'[37] – was a much weightier surety against any pessimism of the intellect or will. For behind it stood the adamantine presence not just of a global movement – the Third International – but of the 'socialist sixth of the world', as the Soviet Union had been dubbed. Like Lincoln Steffens, Hobsbawm and his communist peers thought they had seen the future – and that it worked.[38]

Paradoxically, 1930s communists believed that Stalin's USSR – electrification minus soviets plus terror – embodied 'the legacy of Enlightenment, rationalism, science and progress',[39] and was the ongoing realisation of the traditions and aspirations of a once revolutionary bourgeoisie now shamefully spurned and traduced by its successors. Many British intellectuals in these years had, in effect, turned to communism *because* they were liberals – the message of an influential title published by the Left Book Club in 1937, Stephen Spender's *Forward from Liberalism*. For at stake in the struggle against fascist barbarism was 'the future of a whole civilisation', of which Soviet Marxism was the legitimate inheritor and only true defender: 'If fascism trampled over Marx, it also trampled over Voltaire and John Stuart Mill.'[40] 'Our watchword', in Kiernan's memory of Cambridge communism, 'was Voltaire's: *Ecrasez l'infâme*.'[41] In the 'ideological marriage between "progress" and "revolution"'[42] – as it were, Voltaire, Marx, Mill, Stalin, *même combat*! – Marxism was (as the sub-title of the French journal *La Pensée* had it) 'modern rationalism'.

Reinforcing the trend to Marxism's approximation to 'the old-eighteenth century ideology of progress'[43] was the switch in Comintern policy following the German debacle. Its Seventh Congress in 1935 had formalised the line of 'Popular Frontism', necessitating (as Dimitrov bluntly put it) 'a *definite* choice ... not between proletarian dictatorship and bourgeois democracy, but between bourgeois democracy and fascism' in western Europe.[44] To help create what Hobsbawm has described as 'a set of concentric circles of unity'[45] – united front between communists and socialists, popular front between labour movements and bourgeois liberals, national front of all anti-fascist forces, international front of anti-fascist powers – communists must eschew what Dimitrov castigated as 'national nihilism' and present themselves as champions of their respective nations.[46] For if the 'salvation of the nation' could only ultimately be guaranteed by socialism, fascism doomed it to perdition. Communism was therefore to be aligned, in rhetoric and reality, with the best national traditions in the cause of human progress. The *Internationale*, *Marseillaise* and *Star-Spangled Banner* (if not quite *God Save the King*) could be intoned in unison; the English, American, French and Russian revolutions belonged to one and the same lineage; tricolours were to be assigned their rightful place alongside red flags; and a capacious syllabus of verities stretched from Bacon to Stalin.

Hobsbawm has consistently argued that such selective 'reclamation of patriotism' formed part of a turn that went beyond a purely defensive tactic, amounting to a novel strategy for socialism in circumstances utterly divergent from those of Tsarist Russia.[47] However that may be, it certainly effected a potent fusion between patriotism and a certain internationalism in the context of the international civil war, ideological and military, of the 1930s and '40s. And for the young Hobsbawm it betokened a profound reorientation, to the extent that what Dimitrov had defined as the 'revolutionary realism' of Popular Front politics 'continues to determine my strategic thinking in politics to this day'.[48]

The harvest of Popular Frontism in the 1930s was poor. The 'concentric circles' either failed altogether to materialise – most fatefully, in the case of 'collective security' against German expansionism – or predictably struggled to survive their internal stresses, in the French and Spanish instances. Hobsbawm had been in Paris on Bastille Day in 1936 to witness the massive street celebrations of the previous month's victory by the Popular Front, recalling it as 'one of those rare days when my mind was on autopilot. I only felt and experienced.'[49] Yet the hopes of that year soon turned to ashes; and it would be the overwhelming majority of the National Assembly elected in June 1936, including scores of socialist deputies, that voted full powers to the victor of Verdun four years later. Across the Pyrenees, the Popular Front brought to power in February 1936 was soon confronting a *pronunciamiento* backed by Italy and Germany; and the Spanish Republic was abandoned to its fate by its nominal French *confrère*. Walking in the Pyrenees that summer, Hobsbawm had crossed the border into Puigcerda, where anarchists ruled the roost. Eventually expelled on account of his illegal entry, he retained an abiding memory of the 'tragic farce that was Spanish anarchism'.[50] By contrast, he has always insisted, the Spanish Communist Party possessed the right policy – winning the war as an absolute precondition of making a revolution – but never secured sufficient mass support to implement it effectively. 'What alternative', he asked in 1981, 'was there to the Communist policy in the Spanish Civil War? Then as now, there is only one answer: none.'[51]

The campaign in defence of the Spanish Republic, indelibly symbolised by the International Brigades, has been adjudged by Hobsbawm 'the last and perhaps greatest undertaking of a genuinely international communist movement'.[52] '[T]he only political cause which, even in retrospect, appears as pure and compelling as it did in 1936', it is looked back on 'like the heart-rending and indestructible memory of a first and great love'.[53] And this despite the contribution to its defeat made by the depredations of the Soviet security apparatus, as it transplanted the anti-Trotsky-ist witch-hunt from Eurasia to the Iberian Peninsula, fuelling a civil war within the Civil War that pitted Bakuninite and Marxist imperatives against one another.

Overall, Hobsbawm's reminiscences of the Popular Front era might be reckoned to fail fully to make the transition prescribed by him when writing on Spain in the mid 1960s: 'the time for analysis must succeed that of heroic memories'.[54] By comparison with his analysis of the period of 'class against class', what they are wanting in is precisely that 'realism' about the actual balance of political forces in western Europe to which Hobsbawm, following Dimitrov, so often lays claim. The strategy always contained equal quotients of disingenuity and ingenuousness, if only because many of those beckoned to form the 'circles of unity' were bound to fear communists bearing gifts – a Trojan Horse wherein ostensible defence against fascism secreted actual advance by communism (the burden, naturally shorn of its negative connotations, of Hobsbawm's own interpretation of it).

If 1939 unfolded well for Hobsbawm personally – editorship of *Granta*, election to the Apostles, a starred First in the Tripos winning him a Studentship at King's – politically it brought one disaster after another, culminating in the long-anticipated war. However, this was 'not the war we had expected, in the cause for which the Party had prepared us'.[55] By 1 September, *raison d'état* had prompted the USSR to exchange the chimera of collective security for a Non-Aggression Pact with Germany. But it had also cynically jettisoned the line of anti-fascist unity in the Communist International and instructed the French and British parties that they should oppose any war with Hitler as imperialist. Notwithstanding opposition from senior figures, they loyally executed the about-turn, in the process squandering much of the prestige they had earned in the intervening years.[56] While conceding that the decision 'made neither emotional nor intellectual sense', Hobsbawm observes that he not only 'accepted' it at the time – the alternative, under a regime of 'democratic centralism', would have been resignation or expulsion – but harboured 'no reservations', implying agreement.[57] Comforted in his reaction by the events (and non-events) of the Phoney War, he refers to a 16-page pamphlet, co-authored with Raymond Williams in February 1940, on the Russo-Finnish War, when it briefly looked as if Britain and France might commence hostilities with Nazi Germany by attacking communist Russia.[58] Issued by the Cambridge University Social Club (CUSC), *War on the USSR?* defended the party line on the Winter War, concluding by posting the relevant campaign slogans: 'No Volunteers for Finland. Hands off Russia!'

Called up in February 1940, Hobsbawm's war years – 'the least satisfactory of my life' – were barren,[59] probably less because of his political affiliations (these proved no obstacle to Hill or Saville, Williams or Thompson), than on account of a central European background. Assigned to a sapper regiment, with it Hobsbawm lived the 'extraordinary moment in our history' that was 1940, when, 'standing alone' (albeit with an empire propping the UK up), 'we became a people conscious of our own heroism'.[60] Attesting to the 'patriotism for England' attributed to him by Keunemann, Hobsbawm has elsewhere confided: 'it was clear to me even then that there was an unassuming grandeur about this moment'.[61] ('Unassuming' might not be the first epithet to spring to other minds, even if Hobsbawm is at pains to disown Churchillian bombast.) Identification with the nation was compounded by empathy with the class – the predominantly English workers into whose company Hobsbawm was thrust – as he 'acquired a permanent, if often exasperated, admiration for their uprightness, their distrust of bullshit, their sense of class, comradeship and mutual help'.[62]

Once France had been knocked out and the Battle of Britain begun, the utter unreality and futility of the party's position on the character of the war became ever more apparent.[63] 22 June 1941, which saw Hitler unleash Operation Barbarossa against the USSR, therefore brought a 'sense of relief and hope'. After the interlude of 1939–41, the international communist movement reverted to the line of unity against fascism, with indivisible causes of national liberation and social transformation finding their symbol in Stalingrad, where the tide of war turned. Hobsbawm's personal frustration at drawing a wartime blank, now doubtless all the more acute, was not assuaged by his transfer from the Royal Engineers to act as a sergeant-instructor in the Army Education Corps in the autumn of 1941 (a move that spared him dispatch to Singapore and capture by the Japanese).[64] Confined to a 'curious military limbo', living 'a life of semi-detachment', his disenchanted recollection is that he 'made [no] greater contribution to the political radicalization of the British Army's Southern Command than to the defeat of Hitler'.[65]

Increasingly spending his weekends in London, in May 1943 Hobsbawm married Muriel Seaton, a senior civil servant at the Board of Trade and a party member. This 'helped to clarify my postwar future', prompting an alteration in initial plans for research on the agrarian problem in the Maghreb with a switch to the history of the Fabian Society, the bulk of the sources for which were located in London.[66] Since Hobsbawm's way into the nineteenth-century labour history he subsequently specialised in passed through the Webbs, it was (as he remarked to interviewers in 1978) 'almost by accident ... [that I] began writing about the working class'.[67]

Prior to his demobilisation in February 1946, Hobsbawm had been involved with the anti-Pan German Free Austrian Movement, organised by communists.[68] The shape of the post-war settlement more generally had been the order of the day since 1943, especially given that the dissolution of the Communist International in June 'seemed to put the entire future of the communist movement into question'.[69] The summit between Roosevelt, Stalin and Churchill at Tehran that year held out the prospect of extending the temporary alliance between liberal capitalism and communism into enduring collaboration, once the Axis had been defeated. Hobsbawm claims that the British Communist Party (CPGB) 'based its plans for the future on the assumption that this is what "the Tehran line" meant' and intimates misgivings.[70]

Intellectuals in Arms

In the event, the 'new perspectives', which had seen the CPGB at one stage envisaging continuation of the wartime coalition, rapidly went the way of the hopes and dreams of 1936. By 1948, the Cold War had erupted in Europe and was soon to issue in hot war in Asia. With communists ejected from united front governments in western Europe, and about to wrest a monopoly on power in the eastern half of the continent, the Cominform was established to co-ordinate the communist movement. Zhdanov duly promulgated the line of 'two camps' – bellicose imperialism headed by the USA and irenic socialism fronted by the USSR – dictating a left-turn in communist tactics, from conciliation to confrontation, to split the imperialist camp. Of Hobsbawm's reactions to the events of the first Cold War, *Interesting Times* discloses surprisingly little – not even regarding his response to the momentous advance for communism represented by victory in China in 1949 (which reportedly allowed Pollitt to console himself on a by-election defeat with the thought that 'we may have lost St Pancras, but we've won in China').[71] He had secured a lectureship at Birkbeck in 1947 alongside his distinguished senior comrade J. D. Bernal, and thus just before known (or suspected) communists began to be affected by the bans and proscriptions which, albeit less virulent than in the USA, were operative in the UK. Although Hobsbawm won a fellowship at King's in 1949, and was soon given responsibility for reconstituting the Conversazione Society, during the 1950s he was turned down for several jobs at Cambridge that he obviously anticipated getting, and only promoted to a Readership at Birkbeck in 1959. Worse than any setbacks to his career – indeed, 'my most resented memory of the Cold War' – was the fate of a book on *The Rise of the Wage Worker*, rejected as 'too biased' by the publisher who had commissioned it.[72]

Such individual details – the small change of the global sum – no doubt accentuated the paradox of the period formulated by Hobsbawm: 'what made it easier or, for many, possible to maintain the old faith was, more than anything else, the crusading global anti-communism of the West in the Cold War'.[73] For Hobsbawm these were 'black times, both politically and personally', 1950 marking a nadir with the breakdown of his marriage and the outbreak of the Korean War.[74] Something of their adversity, and the intransigence with which they were met, can be gauged by his coupling of the personal and the political in a pointed question and answer:

'What was more painful: my divorce or the execution of the Rosenbergs, which so many communists at the time felt as a personal defeat and a personal tragedy? It is difficult to separate the two strands that merged in a common mood of determination to survive them.'[75]

While Hobsbawm claims to have welcomed the fact that residence in Cambridge from 1950–55 released him from routine branch duties in London,[76] he was a more than 'dutiful' CP member. The autobiography he penned at his party's request in 1952 testifies to a certain dissatisfaction with his contribution to date.[77] Moreover, an article published in 1954, though obviously for public consumption, betrays no signs of strain in Hobsbawm's relations with his party and thus no hint of the trauma to come. 'Democratic centralism' received a decidedly innocuous gloss:

> There has been very little disagreement on the fundamentals of party policy in the past 10 years, and almost certainly there is no widespread feeling that the machinery for criticism and suggestion is inadequate. ... Executive Committee decisions between congresses arise out of – or are confirmed by – the widest discussion throughout the party, with the result that there is *effective unanimity on all important issues*.[78]

Even now, notwithstanding the recent ravages of Lysenkoism – the two sciences, bourgeois and proletarian – and Zhdanovism – partisanship in philosophy, socialist realism in the arts – the party (so Hobsbawm affirmed) retained its appeal to 'progressive intellectuals', including those attracted by 'the philosophical outlook of Marxism'.[79]

Twelve years later, registering the renewal of the 'dialogue on Marxism' interrupted by the rise of Stalinism, Hobsbawm would concede that during the 'intellectual ice-age' of 1930–56 'very few people ... became communists because of the scientific power of Marx's ideas' – and with good reason:

> Increasingly, we eliminated all elements other than those of Marx, Engels, Lenin and Stalin or what had been accepted as orthodox in the Soviet Union: any theories of art other than 'socialist realism', any psychology other than Pavlov's, even at times any biology other than Lysenko's. Hegel was pushed out of marxism, ... even Einstein roused suspicions, not to mention 'bourgeois' social science as a whole. The more unconvincing our own official beliefs were, the less we could afford a dialogue, and it is interesting that we spoke more often of the 'defence' of marxism than of its power to penetrate.[80]

In conjunction with the *Short Course*, 'compass of communism', Zhdanov's *On Literature, Music and Philosophy*, summoning communists to sectarian rectitude on the cultural front of the Cold War, typified the mindset of the period.[81]

Enemies of NATO, British communists, like their western European comrades, more than ever found themselves *in partibus infidelium* in these embattled years. '[T]he really tough period', Hobsbawm told an interviewer in 2003, 'was the Korean war – there was a war and we were supposed to be on the other side.'[82] And this notwithstanding the studied moderation of the CPGB's Cominformist policy. The first edition of *The British Road to Socialism*, published in January 1951 and cleared by Moscow (if not drafted there), formally presented it. Prioritising the 'restoration of British national independence' surrendered to the USA by Labour and Tories alike, it abrogated the party's previous, more classically Leninist prospectus of the mid 1930s, *For Soviet Britain*.[83] A 'broad popular alliance', led by a 'united working class', would pursue a specifically national strategy for socialism, 'transform[ing] capitalist democracy into a real People's Democracy, transforming Parliament, the product of Britain's historic struggle for democracy, into the democratic instrument of the will of the vast majority of her people'. For all the reformist mutation in programmatic perspectives, however, the Communist Party still possessed its vanguardist *raison d'être*, because '[h]istory proves that without such a party the battle for socialism cannot be won'.[84] The principal obstacle to victory consisted in the Labour Party leadership – hence the bitterness of communist invective against it, which can be sampled in a contemporaneous piece by Hobsbawm excoriating the modern labour aristocracy of Attlee, Bevin and co. as 'a social group whose function is to keep the rank and file firmly tied to the capitalist wagon':

> The stability of capitalist democracy in Britain today depends on the political hold of the Labour Party's leaders on their rank and file. ... The moment when the working-class stands fully exposed

to the winds which blow around the British capitalist economy in its desperate crisis, draws nearer; and with it, the 'crisis of social-democracy', and hence that of the present methods by which the ruling class maintains political control.[85]

The tacit premises underpinning conclusions of this ilk were that capitalism could not fully recover from the near-death experience of the 1930s and that that decade had likewise spelt the doom of 'bourgeois' democracy. Hence the post-war persistence of articles of faith in the 'communist utopianism' enumerated by Hobsbawm in a central chapter of *Interesting Times*, 'Being Communist'. Above all, Marxism of Cold War vintage continued to 'demonstrate with the methods of science the certainty of our victory, a prediction tested and verified by the victory of proletarian revolution over one sixth of the world's surface and the advances of revolution in the 1940s'.[86] Hobsbawm's was what he has called a 'Brechtian generation, which deliberately trained itself to approve the harshest decisions in the war for human liberation'.[87] Brecht's 'wonderful poem *An die Nachgeborenen*', he writes, 'speaks to communists of my generation as no other does'.[88] In so far as it does, it may be said that a leitmotif of his reflection on the communist experience – namely, that 'Communist Parties were not for romantics. ... they were for organization and routine'[89] – represents a unilateral view of it. Such emphasis on 'the Jesuit discipline of the communist parties'[90] is in fact duly qualified in Hobsbawm's subsequent characterisation of the 'Leninist "vanguard party" [as] a combination of discipline, business efficiency, utter emotional identification and a sense of *total* dedication' – an admixture of 'realism' and 'romanticism' evinced in his portrait of 'a hero of our times', Franz Marek.[91]

The bridge between political activism and professional activity from 1946–56 was the Communist Party Historians' Group, in which Hobsbawm participated alongside such figures as Hill, Kiernan, Hilton, Rudé and Maurice Dobb. In historiography as in the national intellectual culture more generally, the 1950s were a time when (as E. P. Thompson memorably put it), 'Napoleonic disenchantment and Victorian conformity [were] telescoped into one. Wordsworth's Solitary and Dickens' Mr. Podsnap ... inhabited a single skin.'[92] The enduring institutional bequest of the Historians' Group was to be the journal *Past and Present*, founded by Hobsbawm with Hill, Hilton and others in 1952. Nailing its colours unapologetically to the mast, until 1957 it advertised itself as 'A Journal of Scientific History', with Ibn Khaldun functioning as *locum tenens* for Marx and Engels, Polybius for Lenin and Stalin, in the shape of selected quotations in the collective editorial that introduced the first number. 'We were ... trying,' Hill et al. later wrote, 'to continue, or to revive, in the post-war period the politics of broad unity we had learned in the days of pre-war anti-Fascism.'[93] Now, as then, the credentials of rationalism were under scrutiny and challenge:

[R]ationalism is the preserve of no creed or party. The present generation, however, has seen the recrudescence of certain schools of thought, descended directly or indirectly from the anti-rational *Weltanschauung* of early nineteenth-century Romanticism, which deny the very possibility of a rational and scientific approach to history. ... We believe that the methods of reason and science are at least as applicable to history as to geology, palaeontology, ecology or meteorology, though the process of change among humans is immensely more complex.[94]

Foremost among the adversaries was Namierism, proudly evacuating history of ideas and reducing high politics to base motives, which epitomised Hobsbawm's contention that 'much modern history is present politics dressed up in period costume'.[95] Whereas it ratified a Burkean conservatism, a national tradition of historical materialism had emerged to inherit and supersede the old liberal-radical interpretation of British history.[96] On this basis Marxist '"popular fronters"' could form 'the spearhead of a broad progressive history ... represented by all manner of radical and labour traditions in British historiography'.[97] That aspiration contained an important epistemological and methodological dimension. It was part and parcel of the broader 'modernisation' of the discipline of history, traditionally political-constitutional in focus and narrative in cast, in which *Annales* was a 'great predecessor' of *Past and Present*.[98] Despite 'patent ideological differences and Cold War polarization', the modernisers were united against a common enemy, identified by Hobsbawm as 'positivism'.[99] As such, they were engaged in the 'battle', symbolised by the names of Namier and Postan,

> between the conventional assumption that 'history is past politics' ...
> and a history of the structures and changes of societies and cultures,
> between history as narrative and history as analysis and synthesis,
> between those who thought it impossible to generalize about human
> affairs in the past and those who thought it essential.[100]

However, for the Marxist party to the 'broad progressive movement' in historiography, substantive issues were of equal, if not greater, moment. Criticising non-Marxist history, counter-posing to it 'politically more radical interpretations',[101] yoking Bunyan's Christian to Tressell's ragged-trousered philanthropist, the communist historians were themselves involved in 'present politics dressed up in period costume': the continuation of Popular Front politics by other – historiographical – means.[102] In the Cold War 'battle of ideas', they regarded themselves as defending not only what a minute of the April 1948 Group meeting termed 'the progressive rationalist tradition',[103] but also the progressive national tradition in British history, descending in an unbroken line of continuity from the 'good old cause' of the seventeenth century. Politicisation and popularisation thus proceeded in tandem with professionalisation. For implicit in seemingly specialist debates about English Absolutism and 'bourgeois revolution',[104] in large part seeded by Dobb's *Studies in the Development of Capitalism* (1946), was a conception of the overall trajectory of modern British history – the role of the people in it (especially in the struggle for democracy), and the role of the (Protestant) English nation in the world, past, present and future.[105]

A collective tribute to Dona Torr, *doyenne* of the historians, in a *Festschrift* to which Hobsbawm contributed, is eloquent testimony to their concerns:

> She made us feel history on our pulses. History was not words on a page, not the goings-on of kings and prime ministers, not mere events. History was the sweat, blood, tears and triumphs of the common people, our people. Above all we learnt from her, with this deep human sympathy for our forefathers, a profound but tempered optimism. The rhythm of history was seen to be not the steady progress upwards of the Victorian Whigs, still less the treadmills of their degenerate successors, but a dialectical process in which gains and loss are two aspects of one movement.[106]

The precise contours of that 'dialectical process' will be examined at greater length in Chapter 2. Suffice it for now to note that the 'continuous Marxist seminar for ourselves' conducted by the Historians' Group,[107] which at one stage planned a collective update of a quintessential product of Popular Frontism, A. L. Morton's *A People's History of England* (1938), was the crucible of Hobsbawm's first edited book – the compilation of documents, commissioned by Torr for a 'History in the Making' series, published in 1948 as *Labour's Turning Point 1880–1900*.[108] However, if his debut conformed to the 'class-struggle analysis' and 'history from the bottom up' in which the distinctiveness of the communist historians' approach has been encapsulated,[109] Hobsbawm remained (as we shall see) a more orthodox Marxist than some of his peers, far less chary about what he once called 'the Marxist *Fragestellung*' outlined in the 1859 Preface, with its schedule of modes of production.[110]

High on that list of questions in the 1940s and '50s, as noted above, was the local instance of 'bourgeois revolution', tabled by Hill's tercentennial pamphlet *The English Revolution 1640*. Revisiting the post-war debates in 1978, Hobsbawm acknowledged that '[o]ur arguments were sometimes designed *a posteriori* to confirm what we already knew to be necessarily "correct"'.[111] Here, at any rate, was a theoretical issue with burning political implications. For were it to be the case that the transition from feudalism to capitalism had not proceeded via a revolution at home, then revolution might not furnish the universally necessary condition not only of that transition, but also – and more importantly – of any future transition from capitalism to socialism. Whatever his second thoughts, in the mid 1950s Hobsbawm subscribed to orthodoxy, nominating England 'the country of the first complete "bourgeois revolution"'.[112] '[E]conomically progressive',[113] for Hobsbawm as for his colleagues the English Revolution thus formed a crucial episode in history essentially conceived as what the youngest member of the group, in a diagnosis of their 'progressivism' and the 'technological humanism' underlying it, characterised as an 'epic', with classes fulfilling (or failing to fulfil) their historically appointed mission. The science of history was pivoted on laws of development: humanity moved forward in a progression from point to point until, with the achievement of socialism, pre-history ended and real history began.[114]

Earthquakes in the East

Dependent upon 'the success of the "Russian experiment"', such progressivism had crystallised in an immediate post-war conjuncture that allowed Hill to pair the USSR and the UK as 'two commonwealths'.[115] A decade later, a trip to the Soviet Union in the winter of 1954–55, in the company of Hill and others at the invitation of the Soviet Academy of Sciences, proved 'dispiriting' for Hobsbawm. This had been his first direct experience of 'really existing socialism' and, although 'politically unchanged', he 'returned ... depressed, and without any desire to go there again'.[116] As to his attitude to developments in the rest of the bloc, in articles contributed to a communist-controlled journal, *New Central European Observer*, from 1948–51, he robustly defended the party line on the 'people's democracies' and cautioned against German revisionism and militarism.[117] In *Interesting Times* he indicates scepticism, hardening into incredulity, about the east European show trials of 1949–52, and sheer disbelief at the precise accusations levelled against Yugoslavia from 1948 and elaborated in Klugmann's mendacious compendium, *From Trotsky to Tito* (1951).[118] None of his fellow historians, he maintains, lent credence to the version of Soviet and CPSU history catechised in the *Short Course* and yet they were oblivious of 'the horrors of the Soviet camps, the extent of which communists did not then recognize'. Unwilling to credit the information available from non-communist sources, even when these were sympathetic to the cause of the October Revolution, and unable to write truthfully about Russia in the twentieth century, the historians steered clear of it.[119] 'Patently,' Hobsbawm writes, 'people like myself did not remain in the Communist Party because we had many illusions about the USSR, although undoubtedly we had some. For instance, we clearly underestimated the horrors of what had gone on in the USSR under Stalin.'[120] If Hobsbawm retained his party card in the 1950s, it was (so he tells us) because a balancing of the geopolitical accounts yielded *un bilan globalement positif*:

> To most of the world, [the USSR] did not seem to be the worst of all possible regimes, but an ally in the fight for emancipation from western imperialism, old and new, and a model for non-European economic and social development. The future of both communists and the regimes and movements of the decolonized and decolonizing world depended on its existence. As far as communists were concerned, supporting and defending the Soviet Union was still the essential international priority. So we swallowed our doubts and mental reservations and defended it.[121]

1956 – a 'traumatic year' in which communists 'lived on the edge of the political equivalent of a nervous breakdown'[122] – brought Khrushchev's 'Secret Speech' at the Twentieth Congress of the CPSU in February, signalling de Stalinisation; and the Soviet suppression of the Hungarian revolution in November, brutally halting it. The impact on the CPGB, as on its west European sister-parties, was dramatic, with around a quarter of the c. 30,000-strong membership eventually quitting.[123] The leadership's futile attempts to conceal Khrushchev's official revelations about Stalin meant that '[w]e were not told the truth about something that had to affect the very nature of a communist's belief'.[124] As chairman of the Historians' Group, Hobsbawm found himself in the eye of the storm. It formed 'the nucleus of vocal opposition to the Party line', for the simple reason that the historians were obliged 'to confront the situation not only as private individuals and communist militants, but in our professional capacity'.[125] The truth about the ensuing events in Hungary was likewise a 'question about history' – history in the making (and unmaking). In a parting of the ways, Saville and Thompson resigned over their refusal to suspend publication of an oppositional journal, *The Reasoner*, in November 1956;[126] Hill followed after the minority report on internal democracy he had signed was overwhelmingly defeated at a Special Congress in April 1957; Kiernan had drifted out by the end of the decade. Together with Dobb and Morton, Hobsbawm was one of the few to stay put. Why?

Following the Russian intervention in Budapest against a movement that was generously socialist in intent, but fatally anti-Soviet in effect, Hobsbawm had signed a sharp collective letter of protest. Published, in a serious breach of discipline, in the *New Statesman* and *Tribune* on 1 December 1956, after the *Daily Worker* had refused to carry it, it is quoted by Hobsbawm in *Interesting Times* as evidence of his opposition to Soviet actions and the CPGB leadership's collusion with them. Its key paragraphs read as follows:

> We feel that the uncritical support given by the Executive Committee of the Communist Party to the Soviet action in Hungary is the undesirable culmination of years of distortion of fact. ... We had hoped that the revelations made at the Twentieth Congress ... would have made our leadership and press realise that Marxist ideas will only be acceptable in the British Labour movement if they arise from the truth about the world we live in.
>
> The exposure of grave crimes and abuses in the USSR, and the recent revolt of workers and intellectuals against the pseudo-Communist bureaucracies and police systems of Poland and Hungary, have shown that for the past twelve years we have based our political analyses on a false presentation of the facts. ...
>
> If the left-wing and Marxist trend in our Labour movement is to win support, as it must for the achievement of socialism, this past must be utterly repudiated. This includes the repudiation of the latest outcome of this evil past, the Executive Committee's underwriting of the current errors of Soviet policy.[127]

Not cited by Hobsbawm was a final rider, advising readers that '[n]ot all the signatories agree with everything in this letter, but all are in sufficient sympathy with its general intention to sign with this reservation'.[128]

Was Hobsbawm among the signatories with reservations? Three weeks before the collective letter was published, but only nine days before it was drafted, a letter from him had appeared in the *Daily Worker* under the headline 'Suppressing Facts' that would suggest as much. It merits quotation at length:

> All socialists ought to be able to understand that a Mindszenty Hungary, which would probably have become a base for counter-revolution and intervention, would be a grave and acute danger for the USSR, Yugoslavia, Czechoslovakia and Rumania which border upon it.
>
> If we had been in the position of the Soviet Government, we should have intervened; if we had been in the position of the Yugoslav Government, we should have approved of the intervention.
>
> But all Socialists ... also understand three other things must be said about the Hungarian situation.
>
> *First*, that the movement against the old Hungarian Government and the Russian occupation was a wide *popular* movement, however misguided.
>
> *Second*, that the fault for creating the situation in which the Hungarian Workers' Party was isolated from, and partly hated by, the people lay with the past policy of the USSR, as well as of the Hungarian Workers' Party.
>
> *Third*, that the suppression of a popular movement, however wrong-headed, by a foreign army is at best a tragic necessity and must be recognised as such.

> While approving, with a heavy heart, of what is now happening in Hungary, we should therefore also say frankly that we think that the USSR should withdraw its troops from the country as soon as this is possible.
>
> This should be said by the British Communist Party publicly if the British people is to have any confidence in our sincerity and judgement. ...
>
> And if they don't follow our lead, how can we hope to help the cause of the existing Socialist States on which we know that Socialism in the world, and in Britain, largely depends?
>
> To admit faults cannot weaken us, and the cause of the USSR, more than it is weakened by issuing statements which all non-Communist readers believe to contain short-sighted and quite unconvincing suppression of fact.[129]

The contrast between Hobsbawm's heavily qualified approval of Soviet actions in the *Daily Worker*, and Thompson's unequivocal condemnation of them in *The Reasoner*, could not be starker. Hobsbawm has often remarked that the lacerations of 1956 did not extend to personal relations between himself and those who resigned from the party.[130] Be that as it may, while he continued his oppositional activity into 1957, in particular as regards inner-party democracy, Hobsbawm manifestly entertained a different historico-political perspective from several of his friends. If the years of automatic solidarity with the Soviet Union came to an abrupt end, he continued to perceive it as a bulwark of international socialism and anti-imperialism – a stance in which he would have been comforted by the other great event of November 1956: the Anglo-French Suez expedition.[131]

Citing Isaac Deutscher's advice to him not to surrender his party card, Hobsbawm writes that, although he heeded it, 1956–57 'convinced [him] that, since the Party had not reformed itself, it had no long-term political future'.[132] Consequently,

> In practice, I recycled myself from militant to sympathizer or fellow-traveller or, to put it another way, from effective membership of the British Communist Party to something like spiritual membership of the Italian CP, which fitted my ideas of communism rather better.[133]

'[I]t was clear to me', he remarked in 1999, 'that the dream was over'.[134] An element of post-lapsarian retro-projection is discernible in such statements,[135] intensifying the puzzle as to why 'it was more important to stay in the CP than not' – something asserted by Hobsbawm on the thirtieth anniversary of 1956, when he told an interviewer that '[w]hatever [the CP's] future may be, I think the net judgement on its role since 1920 in the history of the British working class is enormously positive'.[136] Thus, there was more – much more – to the decision than the admirable loyalty to his own generation of communists professed in 1987 by Hobsbawm, who disdained the ranks of the kind of ex-communist satirised by Edmund Wilson's ditty on Dos Passos ('On account of Soviet knavery/He favors restoring slavery').[137] Over and above any emotional satisfaction that might derive from professional success despite the handicap of party membership, there were rational political grounds for Hobsbawm's decision in whose direction the phrase 'net judgement' points us.

Hobsbawm concludes his treatment of 1956 with the observation that:

> Politically, having actually joined a Communist Party in 1936, I belong to the era of anti-fascist unity and the Popular Front. It continues to determine my strategic thinking in politics to this day. But emotionally, as one converted as a teenager in the Berlin of 1932, I belonged to the generation tied by an almost unbreakable umbilical cord to hope of the world revolution, and of its original home, the October Revolution, however sceptical or critical of the USSR. For someone who joined the movement where I came from and when I did, it was quite simply more difficult to break with the Party than for those who came later and from elsewhere.[138]

Though no doubt part of the answer, even this amounts to too residual a rationale. As we shall see in Chapter 2, Hobsbawm's writings in the 1960s and '70s evince a more positive overall estimate, without any entailment of unconditional or uncritical loyalty, of the past results, present performance and future prospects of international communism by someone who in 1973 unashamedly identified himself as 'a marxist of the "old left"'.[139] If the ties that bound him were not so easily severed, it was because, while the dream may have been over, the USSR no longer a stellar model ('the Soviet Union's today is our tomorrow'), and the 'radiant future' a distant utopia, the reality, however contradictory, was not bereft of potential and promise.

After 1956, in the now 'polycentric' universe of communism, de-Stalinisation was resumed and radicalised by Khrushchev at home. Abroad, the Soviet Union was soon extending uncovenanted support to an episode of completely isolated revolution in the Americas, Castro's Cuba, as to a beleaguered post-colonial regime in Africa, Lumumba's Congo. In western Europe, if one of the mass Communist Parties of the region – the PCF – found itself stalled in the Fifth Republic, the other – the PCI, object of Hobsbawm's affections – appeared an increasingly dynamic force. For its part, the CPGB was stabilised after the exodus of 1956 and staged a recovery. It is therefore no cause for surprise to discover that even as Hobsbawm maintained his links with those who had resigned to found the New Left, immediately contributing to its journals as earnest of collaborative intent,[140] he was briefing King Street on how the party should relate to the *Universities and Left Review* milieu. And the burden of Hobsbawm's assessment – that the movement, while 'unquestionably a real one', was 'extremely confused and unformed..., notably weak on organisation and ideology'[141] – identifies, *a contrario*, what, for all its faults, was present in the Old Left: 'organisation and ideology'.

Like his contemporary Louis Althusser persevering with the PCF in France, or his elder Lukács tolerated by the HSWP in Hungary, Hobsbawm can be seen post-1956 as conducting, *tout compte fait*, a reorientation towards the position of the Western Marxist tradition, which nearly always had a sense of the extent to which the Russian Revolution and its sequels, whatever their barbarities or deformities, represented the sole real breach with the order of capital that the twentieth century has ... seen – hence the ferocity of the onslaughts of the capitalist states against them. ... In the West, moreover, the alternative tradition within the labour movement, that of social-democracy, had lost any force of real opposition to capitalism, becoming a generally servile prop of the status quo. There, the only militant adversaries the local bourgeoisies encountered continued to be Communist Parties ideologically bound to the USSR. ... For all these reasons, the Western Marxist tradition was also typically oblique and prudent in its criticisms of the Communist states themselves.[142]

Less *au-dessus de la mêlée* than in the autobiographer's self-description, the historian not only 'systematically refused to abjure his past',[143] but actively preserved much of it intact into his future. To a greater extent than *Interesting Times* gives us to think, the schoolboy was – remained – father of the man.

2

THE INTERNATIONAL
AND THE ISLAND RACE

With the modulation in the convictions of the political militant, the professional historian was released into his maturity. In the immensely productive decade and a half or so after 1956, Hobsbawm published seven titles bearing his signature: the studies of 'archaic' social movements subsumed under the category of *Primitive Rebels* (1959); the first volume of his history of modernity, *The Age of Revolution* (1962); a selection of essays on labour history, *Labouring Men* (1964); a synthesis of British economic history from the Industrial Revolution, *Industry and Empire* (1968); an analysis of the English agricultural labourers' revolt of 1830, co-authored with George Rudé, *Captain Swing* (1968); an elaboration of the 1959 model of 'primitive' rebellion, *Bandits* (1969); and, finally, the book reviews and articles on communism, Marxism and anarchism collected as *Revolutionaries* (1973).

His first book as such, however, was a survey of *The Jazz Scene*, which appeared in the same year as *Primitive Rebels* under the pseudonym of Francis Newton (after the American trumpeter Frankie

Newton, who happened to be a communist). Doubtless affording him some welcome R&R from the inner-party battles of the time, Hobsbawm had been acting as jazz correspondent for the *New Statesman* since June 1956. Whereas rock music was fully deserving of Marxist disdain for mass culture – 'an art of amateurs and the musically or even the alphabetically illiterate'[1] – jazz did not merit the strictures of an Adorno, who was later taxed with composing 'some of the most stupid pages ever written' on the subject.[2] It was 'a people's music', an authentically popular art guaranteed its place in twentieth-century cultural history in as much as it had 'rescued the qualities of folk-music in a world ... designed to extirpate them; and ... so far maintained them against the dual blandishments of pop music and art-music'.[3] As 'a music of protest and rebellion' by oppressed blacks and whites alike, jazz held a legitimate appeal for communists, who had disregarded Soviet tirades against it even under the Zhdanov dispensation.[4] Indeed, in Hobsbawm's recollection, alluding to an antithesis of broader significance for his sensibility,

> The first really jazz-struck bunch I can recall at Cambridge were those in or on the fringes of the Communist Party in the immediate pre-war years, but whose tastes took them towards the neo-romantic, quasi-surrealist kind of poetry ... [of] the forties: the Rousseauists, rather than the Voltaireans among us.[5]

Spurning the musical culture of a subsequent generation of Rousseauists, the Voltairean critic, albeit targeting what he regarded not so much infamy as inanity, would rashly predict in 1963 that '[i]n 20 years' time nothing of [The Beatles] will survive.'[6]

The Drama of Progress

Despite Hobsbawm's continued subscription to Marxist versions of the Enlightenment progressivism and rationalism he had assimilated in the Popular Front era, *Primitive Rebels* consolidated a contrapuntal preoccupation – in Raphael Samuel's words, 'the historical reconstitution of doomed revolt'.[7] If this was a contrast rather than a contradiction within the overall thrust of his work, it was because (as he told an interviewer in 1986), 'there is ... a subtext [in *Primitive Rebels*] which is a polemic against anarchism and libertarianism ... it was an argument for the *necessity of organisation*'.[8]

Derived from travels to Spain and Italy in the 1950s, frequentation of Italian communist intellectuals (to whom Hobsbawm had been introduced through the good offices of Piero Sraffa) and, via them, the discovery of Gramsci's work, *Primitive Rebels* also had more local origins in contact with social anthropologists (especially Max Gluckman at Manchester University).[9] In studying millenarian movements like the Lazzaretti or Andalusian anarchism, and such phenomena as social bandits or urban riots, the *déformation professionnelle* to be avoided was the condescension, not so much of posterity (as E. P. Thompson put it), as of a desiccated rationality – the 'rationalist and "modernist" bias' that inhibited the *Verstehen* required to do justice to them as 'a sort of "pre-historic" stage of social agitation'.[10] The depth and breadth of Hobsbawm's imaginative empathy with his subjects will be immediately apparent to any reader of his poignant portrait of the Spaniard, Francisco Sabaté Llopart, in *Bandits*. Equally evident, however, are the criteria by which they are ultimately to be judged, as in Hobsbawm's conclusion on Sabate that '[b]y any rational and realistic standards his career was a waste of life'.[11] For the weaknesses of Spanish agrarian anarchists, scouting 'the necessity of organization, strategy, tactics and patience' in their pursuit of the millennium,[12] were fatal.

The explicit normative paradigm of a modern – perhaps even, in the contrast cued by 'primitive', civilised – social movement was the mature labour movement, empowering the exploited and oppressed for the role of potential agents of history as opposed to its perennial victims. In accordance with Marx and Engels's anatomy of the capitalist mode of production, industrialisation was said to have replaced the *menu peuple*, prone to sporadic urban riot, by the industrial proletariat, 'whose very being is organization and lasting solidarity'.[13] Not that revolutionary movements rooted in the industrial working class were lacking in 'that utopianism or "impossibilism" which makes even very modern [revolutionaries] feel a sense of almost physical pain at the realization that the coming of socialism ... will not solve or make soluble *all* problems'. Such impossibilism – hence Hobsbawm's respect for its past incarnations and present manifestations – was probably 'a necessary social device for generating the superhuman efforts without which no major revolution is achieved'.[14] But unless combined with modern ideology, organisation and strategy, its explosive charge was liable to be dissipated, rather than concentrated on the goal of political and social transformation. Inaugurating a new kind of history, the first modern revolutions made a clean break with the past, if not a clean sweep of it:

> The American and French Revolutions ... are probably the first mass political movements in the history of the world which expressed their ideology and aspirations in terms of secular rationalism and not of traditional religion. ... The modern labour movement is the product of this epoch ... because its leading ideology, Socialism ... is the last and most extreme descendant of 18th-century illuminism and rationalism...[15]

Hence a peculiarity of the British labour movement, born in a country whose 'bourgeois revolution' had been fought and won in a pre-modern religious idiom.[16]

It has been said that 'Hobsbawm insists upon facing reality without celebrating it – upon facing what even Marx and Engels often slighted: the tragedy inherent in human progress'.[17] At the time Hobsbawm would almost certainly have denied that the conception of historical progress adopted by the founders of historical materialism slighted the tragedy inherent in it. What he called 'the drama of progress' had met with approval across a wide spectrum of opinion in the nineteenth century. Yet a 'fundamental division' existed 'between those who thought that progress would be more or less continuous and linear, and those (like Marx) who knew that it must and would be discontinuous and contradictory'.[18]

The dividing-line is drawn in *The Age of Revolution* as a sub-division within *the* great ideological divide post-1789 – namely, that between believers in progress and the rest:

> in a sense there was only one *Weltanschauung* of major significance, and a number of other views which ... were at bottom chiefly negative critiques of it: the triumphant, rationalist, humanist 'Enlightenment' of the eighteenth century. Its champions believed firmly (and correctly) that human history was an ascent, rather than a decline or an undulating movement about a level trend. They could observe that man's scientific knowledge and technical control over nature increased daily. They believed that human society and individual man could be perfected by the same application of reason, and were destined to be so perfected by history. On these points bourgeois liberals and revolutionary proletarian socialists were at one.[19]

The former, wedded to the verities of *Manchesterismus*, were justified to a certain extent – 'at this period' – in their belief that capitalism was the ultimate progressive factor in human history. The latter, on the other hand, recast and radicalised Enlightenment, switching the terminus of historical development by designating capitalism a necessary way-station en route to an inevitable socialism. Marxism, as propounded in *The Communist Manifesto*, whose terminology Hobsbawm echoes in the following lines, was the inheritor of the *philosophes*:

> an ideology of progress implies one of evolution, possibly of inevitable evolution through stages of historical development. But it was not until ... Marx ... transferred the centre of gravity of the argument from its rationality or its desirability to its historic inevitability that socialism acquired its most formidable intellectual weapon, against which polemical defences are still being erected. ... capitalism could be shown by means of political economy to possess internal contradictions which inevitably made it at a certain point a bar to further progress and would plunge it into a crisis from which it could not emerge. Capitalism, moreover, ... inevitably created its own grave-diggers, the proletariat .... As capitalism had prevailed, not simply because it was more rational than feudalism, but because of the social force of the bourgeoisie, so socialism would prevail because of the inevitable victory of the workers. It was foolish to suppose that it was an eternal ideal. ... It was the child of capitalism. It could not even have been formulated in an adequate manner before the transformation of society which created the conditions for it. But once the conditions were there, the victory was certain, for [in the words of Marx's 1859 Preface] 'mankind always sets itself only such tasks as it can solve'.[20]

Exposition without defence but suggesting adherence, and repeatedly sounding the note of ineluctability, this passage may be regarded as a profession of faith by Hobsbawm in the progressive trajectory of history outlined by Marx's 1859 Preface, which 'presents historical materialism in its most pregnant form'.[21]

Introducing an English translation of the section of the *Grundrisse* devoted to 'pre-capitalist economic formations' in 1964, Hobsbawm noted that:

> The *Formen* seek to formulate the content of history in its most general form. This content is *progress*. Neither those who deny the existence of historical progress nor those who ... see Marx's thought ... as an ethical demand for the liberation of man, will find any support here. For Marx progress is something objectively definable, and at the same time pointing to what is desirable.[22]

However – a critical caveat – it was mistaken to attribute to Marx a unilinear conception of historical development, or the simplistic view that it was 'a mere record of progress'. Marx's characterisation of successive modes of production as 'progressive' in the 1859 Preface entailed nothing more than the contention that each of them was 'in crucial respects further removed from the primitive state of man', registering greater emancipation from nature with growing control over it thanks to the expansion of human productive powers.[23]

Accordingly, the 'materialist conception of history' was one in which history is directional, not cyclical; and progressive, not regressive. Yet the pattern of that progress was neither unilinear nor rectilinear, but a discontinuous, 'dialectical' process wherein history could (so Marx insisted contra Proudhon) advance by the 'bad side' – indeed, invariably did.[24] In the properly Marxian assessment of the role of capitalism in history, it was (as Fredric Jameson has aptly put it) 'at one and the same time the best thing that has ever happened to the human race, and the worst'.[25] Any unilateral estimate of it failed to capture the contradictoriness of capitalism as a historical phenomenon. To perceive only its negative aspects was to succumb to Romanticism, harking back to some mythical golden age. To ignore them was to lapse into the callous utilitarianism of the 'bourgeois viewpoint', transubstantiating 'times of iron and fire' (to borrow a phrase from Gramsci) into the golden age. Marx's causal explanation of the origins and dynamics of the capitalist mode of production issued in an evaluation of it as at once creating the emancipatory promise of modernity and obstructing it. The full potential of modernity could only be realised by revolution in its modern sense of comprehensive transformation – the ambition of the 'scientific socialism' that sought to prepare the future by understanding the present; interpreting the world aright in order to change it for the better.

As regards the appraisal of capitalism in the Marxist tradition after Marx, we can identify three broad tendencies, two of which revolve around what he called the 'antithesis' between 'romantic' and 'bourgeois' standpoints (*le dur commerce, le doux commerce*).[26] The first – the Romantic anti-capitalism represented by the early Lukács and Frankfurt School, and subsequently instantiated by under-development theorists like Andre Gunder Frank or Samir Amin (by Third Worldism, as it were, out of Russian Populism) – adjudged capitalism an unmitigated disaster. The second – the neo-utilitarian pro-capitalism espoused, for example, by Legal Marxism in Tsarist Russia and Bill Warren in Britain in the 1970s – deemed it an unqualified blessing. The third – the equipoise inherited from Marx and Engels by Lenin and Trotsky, Luxemburg and Gramsci – aimed to surmount any such antithesis intellectually, while pointing to its transcendence practically. In so doing, it likewise dispensed with what Hobsbawm has called 'the simple dichotomies of those who set out to replace the bad society by the good, unreason by reason, black by white'.[27] Capitalism was an irreducibly contradictory reality, its essential dynamic one of creative destruction. Above all – communist consequence and corollary of the capitalist present – it had a superior societal future ahead of it, generating the material and social preconditions for its own supersession, as the sorcerer unwittingly conjured up the gravedigger. Thus conceived, it constituted a tragic process that nevertheless represented Promethean progress. Marx's reckoning of the impact of British imperialism on India can, minus the allusion to 'the most advanced peoples', be taken to encapsulate Hobsbawm's settled, classically Marxist outlook:

> When a great social revolution shall have mastered the results of the bourgeois epoch, the market of the world and the modern powers of production, and subjected them to the common control of the most advanced peoples, then only will human progress cease to resemble that hideous pagan idol, who would not drink the nectar but from the skulls of the slain.[28]

Here was what Maurice Dobb et al., extolling Dona Torr's contribution to their intellectual formation, had identified as 'a dialectical process in which gains and loss are two aspects of one movement'.[29] The potential pitfalls of such a conception of historical progress are readily apparent. They were duly attested by the Stalinist exaltation of the inexorable advance of the productive forces – a technological humanism to which nothing inhuman was alien – satirised by E. P. Thompson's verse on the Emperor of Ch'in ('However many the emperor slew/The scientific historian/(while taking note of contradiction)/Affirms productive forces grew'). For Hobsbawm, however, enthusiastically greeting E. H. Carr's *What is History?* as 'a powerful and brilliant salvo fired against historical obscurantism',[30] the issue was not in doubt. The batteries of post-war historiographical conservatism had been trained on 'a sort of historical popular front' that included Marxism but ranged far beyond it:

> All liberal and radical history in the old-fashioned sense, all history which believed that man's evolution is a progress, all history which attempted to apply reason and science to the past, or which believed that its investigation could help us to understand and master present and future, were equally dismissed.[31]

Historical materialists would 'rejoice in seeing that those who share [their] views are once again on the offensive'.[32]

Like *The Age of Revolution*, 'Progress in History' was written at the height of Khrushchevite reformism in the USSR, against the backdrop of Soviet satellites and manned space flights, no doubt facilitating Hobsbawm's striking reaffirmation later the same year that the Russian Revolution alone 'provided the means and the model for genuine world-wide economic growth and balanced development of all peoples'.[33]

Marx's views on historical progress had taken shape in the context of the consummation of agrarian capitalism and the consolidation of industrial capitalism in England. Hobsbawm's attunement to the 'bad side' of the 'commercial society' lauded by its champions is clear from his treatment of the victims of both. Thus, in *Labouring Men* he remonstrated with the 'whitewashing of early industrial Britain' by the editors of a new edition of Engels's *The Condition of the Working Class in England*, castigating 'the lack of historical or human imagination and realism' typical of those who took an optimistic view of the impact of the Industrial Revolution.[34] 'So far as the victims ... were concerned,' he wrote,

> the results were as bad as – perhaps worse than – if they had been achieved by deliberate cruelty: inhuman, impersonal, callous degradation of the spirit of men and women and destruction of their dignity. Perhaps this was historically inevitable and even necessary. But the victims suffered. ... And any historian who cannot appreciate this is not worth reading.[35]

In his own initial intervention in the 'standard of living debate', Hobsbawm had defended the traditional – bleak – view associated with J. L. Hammond, regretting the fact that the latter had gratuitously conceded the statistical case to the chief optimist, John Clapham, and shifted his ground to 'moral and other non-material territories'. Detailed examination of the 'quantitative evidence' vindicated the pessimists, who could therefore dispense with imponderable claims about the quality of life in the first half of the nineteenth century.[36] In a Postscript, while recording his satisfaction that the burden of statistical disproof had reverted to the optimists, Hobsbawm retracted the narrowly quantitative focus of his earlier contribution. Invoking Karl Polanyi on the 'catastrophic dislocation of the lives of the common people' brought about by industrialisation, he urged a return to 'the wider and more sensible perspective of the pre-Claphamite historians'. For to conduct the controversy exclusively in terms of real incomes and other such indicators was to risk 'diverting us from the real historical problem which the original observers of the Industrial Revolution and the classical historians saw, but the "optimists" have failed to see. The effects of the Industrial Revolution on the labouring poor are both economic ... and social.'[37]

Polanyi's *The Great Transformation* had been commended in the bibliography of *The Age of Revolution*, for its corroboration of Hobsbawm's searing verdict on the ravages visited by the intrusion of liberal imperatives into European rural economies, delivered in an unforgettable simile: 'like some form of silent bombardment which shattered the social structure he [the peasant or cottager] had always inhabited and left nothing in its place but the rich: a solitude called freedom'.[38] Polanyi's 'brilliant and unduly neglected book' informed Hobsbawm's and Rudé's analysis of the desperate resistance mounted by English farm-labourers to the full impact of rural capitalism in *Captain Swing*.[39] 'It is difficult', they wrote, 'to find words for the degradation which the coming of industrial society brought to the English country labourer. ... They did not even sell their birthright for a mess of pottage. They simply lost it.'[40]

Proletarianisation and pauperisation were not simply the result of some impersonal law of political economy, but the direct, intended consequence of ruling-class policy, exemplified by the 'inhuman statute' that was the New Poor Law, and which 'destroyed the last and most modest of [the labourers'] claims on society, namely the belief that it would not let poor men starve like dogs'.[41] At work was a process whose ineffability found due expression in accents of *saeva indignatio*, involving as it did

> the systematic and growing degradation of the labourers by their rulers, who sought to turn them into a class of helpless and abject helots, and rural society into a racialist structure distinguished from the others so dear to the Victorian upper classes by the fact that the lower races happened also to be white.[42]

As to the 1830 uprising itself, the 'improvised, archaic, spontaneous movements of resistance', aimed at putting an end to unemployment and wresting a living wage, had missed their rendezvous with the contemporaneous 'rebellion of mine, mill and city'.[43] Unorganised, isolated, repressed, the farm-labourers subsequently experienced a 'modernization of their intellectual universe' whose fruit, in the 1870s, was a 'modern movement' on a national scale.[44] Therewith, as in the case of those other 'helots' – the victims of imperialism – the tables might eventually be turned. Where resistance in the name and in defence of tradition was doomed to defeat, resistance 'with the weapons of progress itself'[45] enjoyed better prospects of success.

In any event, a genuinely exacting social history was obliged to avoid the vices reproved by Hobsbawm in some subsequent 'people's history', much of it directly or distantly influenced by Thompson's *The Making of the English Working Class* (1963).[46] Intended to inspire,

> The problem about this kind of history ... is that it sacrifices analysis and explanation to celebration and identification. It encourages a vogue for antiquarianism ... and for a dislike of generalisation which in itself is no more satisfactory in red versions than in true-blue ones.[47]

If, as Hobsbawm phrased the desideratum in a programmatic article from 1970, a transition must be made 'from social history to the history of society', it was so that historians might become fully contemporary with Marx, 'the thinker who, more than any other, has defined or suggested the set of historical questions' dominating the agenda of the social sciences at the close of the 1960s.[48] First and foremost among them – 'the $64 billion question of history', as Hobsbawm denominated it much later, in the idiom of his New York audience – was 'how to explain the complex, uneven, interlacing path of global human development from the palaeolithic to the nuclear era, through a variety of forms of social organization'.[49] This was 'what history in the broadest sense is about'.[50] But it did not exclude other histories – of all those vanquished in the tragic drama and unredeemed time of *homo sapiens*' epochal progress. These remained to be written.

Observation and Participation

Reviewing Perry Anderson's *Considerations on Western Marxism* in 1976, Hobsbawm queried one of the defining characteristics it predicated of the tradition: 'these writers share not so much "a common and latent pessimism" ... as a disenchanted hope, a political will and passion matured – he is one of the few to recognise this – by a *sense of history as a tragic process*'.[51] In writing thus, Hobsbawm might also have been penning a laconic self-description 15 years or so after the remarkable efflorescence of Marxism in the 1960s, which made for such a positive contrast with 'the tone of anti-Marxism in that discouraging decade', the 1950s.[52] Urging Marxism 'to liquidate the heritage of the sort of intellectual ice-age through which it passed' after the rise of Stalin, in 1966 he remarked that 'a general trend towards marxism is combined with a disintegration of the traditional marxist analysis'.[53] In the wake of what might more accurately be described as a disintegration of the orthodox Marxist-Leninist analysis, and termination of the quasi-automatic equation it imposed between communism and Marxism, the latter likewise became pluralist and 'polycentric'.[54] During the 1960s and '70s, developments in both were to be tracked by Hobsbawm in his capacity as 'a modest participant' or 'participant observer'.[55]

Hobsbawm's intermittent engagement with the Western Marxist tradition at the moment of its rediscovery and final burst of productivity offers valuable evidence as to his own brand of historical materialism. Profound scepticism about the credentials of Existential Marxism is apparent from a glancing allusion to Sartre's *Critique of Dialectical Reason* (1960).[56] An allergy to Critical Theory (if only on account of its antipathy to jazz?) may be inferred from his silence about it, even as *Dialectic of Enlightenment* (1944) was being republished in West Germany and translated into English. A sympathetic sketch of the dilemma confronted by Karl Korsch, anti-revisionist but anti-Bolshevik, concluded with unsparing criticism of 'an ideological St. Simeon on his pillar'.[57] On the other hand, Ernst Bloch's *The Principle of Hope* (1959), for all that it was 'strange, overcrowded, sometimes absurd', was greeted as a 'superb work', potent antidote to the end-of-ideology theorists of the 1950s: 'it is not every day that we are reminded ... that hope and the building of the earthly paradise are man's fate'.[58]

Manifest admiration for 'a sort of marxist Schelling' notwithstanding,[59] Hobsbawm's own historical and political concerns led him in different directions. Given the widespread tendency at the time to counter-pose the young Marx's ethical philosophy of history not only to Stalinism, but also to the historical materialism of the mature Marx and Lenin, Althusser's ambitious reconstruction of Marx's intentionally scientific theory of history in *For Marx* and *Reading Capital* (1965) was to be welcomed.[60] Even so, Hobsbawm's reservations, spelt out in his review article and a contribution to a conference to mark the centenary of *Capital*, were profound. Historical materialism was indeed in some sense a 'structural-functionalist theory of society' and Marx 'a structuralist *avant la lettre*'.[61] However, their distinctiveness was twofold. First, as indicated by the base/superstructure topography, Marx had postulated a hierarchy in the plurality of social levels, prioritising the economic mode of production. Consequently, while his theory was not one of 'universal unilinear evolution', it did attribute a 'direction' to the course of history. Second, Marx had identified 'internal contradictions' – in particular, that between the forces and relations of production – as the mechanism of epochal historical transformation, or the transition from one mode of production to another.[62] On the Marxian interpretation, history was not merely *process* but *progress*. This was the core of Hobsbawm's objections to Althusser's particular anti-evolutionistic recasting of historical materialism, licensed by the permissive protocols of 'symptomatic reading' that 'allow[ed] Althusser to say what [Marx] ought to have said'.[63] Structural-functionalism seemed to provide a means of liberating [Marxism] from the characteristic evolutionism of the nineteenth century, with which it was so often combined, though at the cost of also liberating it from the concept of 'progress' which was also characteristic of nineteenth-century thought, including Marx's. But why should we wish to do so? Marx himself certainly would not have wished to do so. … In certain respects, which Marxists and common sense regard as crucial, such as the control of man over nature, it certainly implies unidirectional change or progress, at least over a sufficiently long time-span.[64]

In allocating explanatory primacy to the relations of production and effectively downgrading the productive forces to a sub-set of them, Althusser had implicitly expelled the 1859 Preface from the Marxist canon. Yet this was the text which (as Hobsbawm put it on the centenary of Marx's death) provided 'the fullest formulation' of historical materialism, prompting the question as to 'whether one can reject it and remain a Marxist'.[65]

Althusser's subsequent intellectual trajectory held no attractions for Hobsbawm, who in 1966 feared that the emergent Althusserian school would not descend from 'the heights of what one might call meta-history' and in 1990 reported confirmation of his worst fears.[66] Hobsbawm's brusque, indiscriminate dismissal of the Marxism produced in France from 1968 is a travesty, suggesting a less than passing acquaintance with it. But be that as it may, his hostility to its Althusserian strain was doubtless informed by political considerations, as the 'ideological hard-liner' detected by him moved closer to Maoism and (in Hobsbawm's view) therewith reverted to variations on 'the simple primary-school marxism of the old days' taught in Beijing.[67]

The alternative to Maoism was certainly not to be found in the contemporaneous revival of Trotskyism in the west, not even in the guise of such outstanding representatives as Isaac Deutscher. Intellectually, the Trotskyist tradition had shown itself 'quite unable to transcend the historical framework of the communist discussions in the USSR of the 1920s'.[68] For a pioneering theory of politics consonant with modern western realities, Marxists must turn elsewhere – to Gramsci, 'the most original [Marxist] thinker produced in the west since 1917'.[69]

Writing in *Marxism Today* in 1977, Hobsbawm rejoiced that 'Gramsci has become part of our intellectual universe.'[70] As we have indicated, he had become part of Hobsbawm's a quarter-century earlier, when he had been one of the first Anglophone intellectuals to discover the Sardinian's conceptual repertoire in the edition of the *Prison Notebooks* assembled after the war by the Italian Communist leader, Palmiro Togliatti. Hobsbawm was the sole British representative at the Congress of Gramsci Studies in Rome in January 1958;[71] and presumably played some part in the decision of Lawrence and Wishart to publish an initial selection from the *Notebooks* in 1957 as *The Modern Prince and Other Writings*. (It was translated by his friend Louis Marks, a member of the Communist Party Historians' Group.)

Gramsci formed a striking contrast to the other main communist theorists in the Western Marxist tradition, Lukács and Althusser, both of them marginal figures in their parties, whose work was regarded with deep suspicion by their leaders. His intellectual legacy, in the official version of it at any rate, had been a living force in the thinking of his party since its refoundation in the Resistance. Hobsbawm's endorsement of the theory was well-nigh inseparable from his espousal of the practice. Endowed with 'an unusually able party leadership', the PCI (he wrote in 1972) was 'the great success story in the history of communism in the western world, or that part of it in which such parties are not in power'.[72] Why? Because since 1944 it had consistently demonstrated its ability creatively to address the overriding dilemma facing European communism virtually from its inception – namely, how parties established to lead socialist revolutions should operate in advanced capitalist countries whose political and social environment was inimical to successful insurrection on the classical (i.e. Bolshevik) model.[73] Contrary to the superannuated Trotskyist thesis of Stalinist betrayal, the PCI had been right not to attempt to seize power in 1944–45. Thereafter, declining to bunker down into an impotent maximalism, while seeking to elude the lures of a minimalist gradualism, it had embarked on a *terza via* between Leninism and social-democracy, geared towards 'a transition to socialism in conditions other than the historically exceptional ones of the years after 1917'.[74] In the process, it had remained a mass party –

by far the largest in western Europe – expanded as an electoral force, proved itself in local government, and exercised something approaching intellectual hegemony in the first Italian Republic.

The relevant foil here was not the small CPGB, which faced a more acute version of the common west European predicament given that Britain 'lack[ed] even a living tradition of past revolutions',[75] but the PCF, functioning in a country replete with them. French communism's post-war record was vitiated by a persistent 'workerism' that had seen it indulge in the worst excesses of Zhdanovism and Lysenkoism; and a recurrent sectarianism, which preserved its identity at the cost of squandering such rare political opportunities as arose in the Fifth Republic – for example, in May 1968, when it had failed the test as a reformist party, let alone a revolutionary one.[76] Its immobilism had met with condign punishment, summarised by Hobsbawm in 1990: 'The Communist party maintained itself for a generation within a sort of ghetto or fortress, whose defences kept the intrusions of the late twentieth century at bay, but its own decline in the 1980s was all the more spectacular.'[77]

Whatever the justice of this inclement account – astigmatic in more than one aspect – it stands in stark contrast to Hobsbawm's leniency towards the subsequent evolution of the PCI, whose self-dissolution and successive reinventions in ever more ignominious forms from the 1990s are blandly registered (if not altogether exculpated) in *Interesting*

Times as 'abandoning too much of a great tradition with its name'.[78] In fact, qualifying if not contradicting the positive drift of Hobsbawm's estimate of Italian communism are some stray remarks by him on *its* failure to act as a radically reformist party when it had the chance – in the immediate post-war period, when it stayed its hand against the Catholic Church and the state apparatus inherited from fascism, the very 'institutions which were, in effect, to push it into the political wilderness after 1948'.[79]

The point had been raised in the long interview with the then leader of the PCI right and current President of Italy, Giorgio Napolitano – a close personal friend – in 1977, at the height of Eurocommunism.[80] A misnomer for a phenomenon that encompassed the Japanese Communist Party, for example, but definitely not the proudly traditionalist Portuguese and Greek parties, Eurocommunism briefly saw the Italian, French and Spanish CPs more or less aligned in their quest for a peaceful and democratic road to socialism.[81] Despite his warm support for it as a continuation of Popular Front traditions, Hobsbawm posed one of the burning questions tabled by Eurocommunism:

> if one foresees a transition to socialism which passes through bourgeois democracy in an infinite series of steps, how does one avoid falling into a Social Democratic conception? In short, what about the question: wasn't the PCI beginning to turn itself into just another reformist, gradualist party, into a new type of Fabianism?[82]

In the event, the Eurocommunist strategy was never fully put to the question in southern Europe as the PCI, PCF and PCE, each in its different way, lost out to reminted Eurosocialist parties that would govern their respective countries in the 1980s. The Italian variant of it had been justified by the *dénouement* of the Popular Unity experiment in Chile, closely monitored from the outset by Hobsbawm.

Santiago was a crucial testing-ground, because 'Chile is the first country in the world that is seriously attempting an alternative road to socialism.'[83] By dint of this – '[j]ust because Chile may actually be a model for other countries' – even the most sympathetic observers were on notice to examine developments 'coldly and realistically'. Predictably pointing to the Communist Party as 'the core of the UP and by far its most effective and rational component', Hobsbawm anticipated an eventual clash between Allende and his opponents, while surmising that it might assume a different form from the invasion or military coup projected by 'ultra-left apocalyptics'. A coup d'état was a possibility, but the Chilean armed forces were restrained not so much by their respect for the constitution – although that did exist – as by 'the knowledge that it would lead to civil war'. Even so, the odds were weighted against this experiment in democratic socialism.

Two years on, and an obituary of it was bound to remark that '[h]owever tragic the news of the coup, it had been expected and predicted. It surprised nobody.' As if forgetful of his dismissal of 'ultra-left apocalyptics',

Hobsbawm now warned that '[t]he left has generally underestimated the fear and hatred of the right, the ease with which well-dressed men and women acquire a taste for blood'. In the face of that reality, however, he could urge nothing more than a velleity: 'to those … who asked what other choice remained open to Allende's opponents but a coup, the simple answer is: not to make a coup'.[84]

By the end of the 1970s, then, the reformist road to socialism had ended in an impasse in western Europe and Latin America alike. In the interim, what the Austrian communist Ernst Fischer dubbed *Panzerkommunismus* had put paid to Czech 'socialism with a human face', terminating any further de-Stalinisation in the eastern bloc for close on two decades. Condemned by the Italian and British CPs among others – Hobsbawm's agreement can be taken as read – the suppression of the Prague Spring by the armies of the Warsaw Pact in August 1968 had nourished Eurocommunism, initiating a western schism in the international communist movement that compounded the eastern schism effected by the Sino-Soviet split of the early 1960s. What Hobsbawm retrospectively characterised as 'the tragic occupation of Czechoslovakia by the USSR'[85] confirmed the underlying lesson drawn from 1956 by someone not tempted to embrace Mao's China, then in the throes of a disastrous Cultural Revolution blithely idealised by many, as a model for a desirable and viable socialism. As he observed in a balance-sheet of *Marxism Today* in 1982:

1956 marks the beginning of a period in which the majority of Marxists were forced to conclude that the existing socialist regimes ... were far from being what might be desired as a socialist society or a society that had embarked on the construction of socialism. The majority of Marxists were obliged to revert to the position adopted by socialists before 1917. They once again had to conceive of socialism as the requisite solution to the problems created by capitalist society, as a hope for the future, but as something that had very little adequate support in practical experience. This did not necessarily lead them to underestimate the notable and, in many respects positive, results of the attempts hitherto made to build socialism in the face of great difficulties...[86]

Of course, 1968 had been the year not only of the Prague Spring in the Second World, but the Vietnamese Tet Offensive in the Third and the French May in the First. Contrary to the relentlessly negative retrospect of *Age of Extremes* and *Interesting Times* (to which we shall return in Chapter 3), Hobsbawm had shared at least some of the hopes of the time for other – better – socialisms. The start of the year had found him in Havana for a cultural congress on which he reported back enthusiastically. In 1960 he had celebrated a 'remarkably endearing and encouraging revolution', while cautioning against 'an access of Cubatopianism'.[87] Eight years later, the Havana gathering was offered as welcome evidence that '[t]he situation of the 1950s has been reversed', representing as it did a kind of counter-Congress for Intellectual Freedom and renaissance of the *engagement* of the 1930s. The country in which it was held was not only 'embattled and heroic', but 'remarkably attractive'.[88] Not that Castroism was to be misconstrued as a species of libertarianism. The image of Che Guevara being circulated across the world, in the wake of his ill-starred Bolivian expedition of 1967, was a romantic and – correspondingly – erroneous one.[89]

As early as 1965, Hobsbawm had banked on a US defeat in Vietnam at the hands of a communist revolutionary movement fusing the goals of national liberation and social transformation.[90] Accordingly, the Tet Offensive may be reckoned to have come as much less of a surprise than the May Events in France which it, and the campaign against the Vietnam War (in which Hobsbawm actively participated), did so much to stimulate. Invited to react to the events as they were unfolding, Hobsbawm, who chanced to be in Paris for the UNESCO conference on Marx as the barricades were going up, for once publicly wore his heart on his sleeve:

> What has happened in France is marvellous and enchanting. ... Does it show the way to the rest of the world? It would not be the first time that Paris has done so. I think it may do so now. The events in France are unexpected and totally unprecedented ... What France proves is that when someone demonstrates that people are *not* powerless, they may begin to act again. Perhaps even more than this: that only the sense of impotence is holding many of us back from acting like men and not zombies.[91]

In a subsequent, more considered reflection *post festum*, Hobsbawm noted that May 'seemed to demonstrate what practically no radical over the age of twenty-five ... believed, namely that revolution in an advanced industrial country was possible in conditions of peace, prosperity and apparent political stability'.[92] If the situation had not in fact been classically revolutionary, it might have developed in that direction. However, this had been prevented by the ideological gulf between students and workers (whose decisive general strike had for the most part been neglected in the outpouring of literature post-May), the political sterility of the PCF, and – a factor certainly not to be underestimated – the all too contrasting brilliance of de Gaulle.

The most spectacular episode in a bi-continental student revolt either side of the Atlantic (and in both halves of Europe), May '68 marked the zenith of the New Left almost unremittingly disparaged by the historian of the short twentieth century and the auto-biographer. The participant observer had been more nuanced. In 1961, reviewing Bloch, he evoked 'the passionate, turbulent, confused but hopeful atmosphere of that international phenomenon, the intellectual "new left"'.[93] Its effervescence proved that the concerted efforts of the Cold War liberals in the 1950s to instil 'despair or scepticism' had come to naught. On the other hand – and here was the rub:

> The impressive 'new left' of recent years is admirable, but in many respects it is not only new, but also a regression to an earlier, weaker, less developed form of the socialist movement, unwilling or unable to benefit from the major achievements of the international

working-class and revolutionary movements in the century between the Communist Manifesto and the Cold War.[94]

Compared with their elders from the 1930s, the new generation of revolutionaries in the west, *de jure* Marxist but *de facto* Bakuninite, had emerged in the context of the 'sensational success' of post-war capitalism in developing the productive forces and delivering relative material prosperity (or a realistic prospect of it in the foreseeable future).[95] In these circumstances, the traditional Marxist indictment of the irrationality and inhumanity of the capitalist economy – for its endemic crises and exploitation/'pauperisation' of workers – had mutated into a sociological critique of the 'alienation' and 'bureaucratisation' of advanced capitalist society.[96] Symptomatic of the substitution of alienation for exploitation as grounds for youth (and not so youthful) revolt was the ubiquitous but fallacious connection made between political and social revolution, on the one hand, and sexual liberation, on the other. This libertarian – even antinomian – dimension to the New Left's cultural rebellion received short shrift just as the age of Aquarius was dawning: 'Shocking the bourgeois is, alas, easier than overthrowing him.'[97]

What, above all else, fundamentally distinguished the New Left from the Old was this:

> We had, perhaps mistakenly, hope and a concrete model of the alternative society: socialism. Today this faith in the great October revolution and the Soviet Union has largely disappeared ... and nothing has replaced it. For though the new revolutionaries are

looking for possible models, neither small and localized revolutionary regimes – Cuba [etc.]... – nor even China, have provided an equivalent for what the Soviet Union was in my time. What has taken the place of our perspective is a combination of negative hatred of the existing society and Utopia.[98]

At the hands of the class of '68, socialism had thus become utopian once again – less Marx's '*real* movement which abolishes the present state of things' than, say, Fourier's '*state of affairs* which is to be established, an *ideal* to which reality will [have] to adjust itself'.[99]

In the same 1971 article as Hobsbawm diagnosed this 'relapse' among students and intellectuals, he raised the possibility of another, no less disabling one in the ranks of workers: the regression of their movement to a 'militant and powerful', but nevertheless restricted, 'economism'.[100] By the end of the decade, the theme had moved centre-stage in his writings on British politics.

Divisions of Labour

Prefacing the studies collected in *Labouring Men* in 1964, Hobsbawm distinguished their approach to the subject from the kind of narrative labour history associated with the Webbs and G. D. H. Cole, remarking that there had hitherto been 'comparatively little work about the working classes as such (as distinct from labour organizations and movements), and about the economic and technical conditions which allowed labour movements to be effective, or which prevented them from being effective'.[101] If, in a subsequent collection – *Worlds of Labour* (1984) – Hobsbawm could note with satisfaction that '[t]he past twenty years have undoubtedly been a golden age for labour history',[102] it was in no small measure thanks to his contribution to overcoming the tendency to identify the history of the class with the history of its movements. Some amends for another ingrained tendency in labour history – the glaring omission of working women – would only be made much later.[103]

In so far as the ultimate goal of Hobsbawm's work in this area was (as he put it in 1974) 'to create a world in which working people can make their own life and their own history',[104] the effectiveness (or ineffectiveness) of labour movements was of course a major issue. Before turning to the British case, we must highlight a problem that might be seen as the political equivalent of the historiographical 'substitutionism' referred to above. According to Hobsbawm, the working class in-itself (to employ classical Marxist terms) only became a class for-itself – a collective 'subject of history' – when institutionally organised. Consequently, as in some iron law of oligarchy, the danger of substitutionism was ever-present: 'Organizations, which give reality to "the people", class or group, are by definition superimposed on them, and tend to substitute themselves for their members.'[105] Quoting Trotsky's critique of Bolshevism in *Our Political Tasks* almost verbatim, though without acknowledgement, Hobsbawm ventured that some degree of 'divergence' between class, movement, party and leadership was 'inevitable'. This had significant implications for how socialism was conceived. Contrary to Marx, it could not straightforwardly be construed as working-class self-emancipation:

> The crucial problem for socialists is that revolutionary socialist regimes ... arise not out of class, but out of the characteristic combination of class and organization. It is not the working class itself which takes power and exercises hegemony but the working-class movement or party, and (short of taking an anarchist view) it is difficult to see how it could be otherwise.[106]

Firmly Leninist and Gramscian in self-conception, such considerations could offer an alibi for Stalinism – and had.

What, then, of the British working class and its movement? The basic fact here was the fundamental break in the history of both. With the successful negotiation of the crisis over parliamentary reform in the early 1830s, repeal of the Corn Laws and end of the 'hungry forties', the spectre of revolution haunting propertied Britain after the Napoleonic Wars was dispelled. Chartism subsided; socialism 'disappeared from the country of its birth'.[107] The pioneering industrial-capitalist power, achieving global economic domination by virtue of its monopoly as 'workshop of the world', attained its meridian. Therewith the working class made by the Industrial Revolution – the subject of Thompson's great book – was re-made, as it confronted an economic system that seemed to be a permanent fixture, rather than a passing aberration. What came to be thought of as the 'traditional' manual working class in the 1950s and '60s was new in the 1880s, formed in and by these circumstances. It was broadly divided into a skilled minority, organised in craft unions and enjoying a sellers' market, and an unskilled mass, largely unorganised and subsisting in a buyers' market. It was, and for well over 50 years remained, relatively homogeneous socially and culturally, a separate (even segregated), self-consciously proletarian estate that formed a majority of the British population – 'a single working class, bound together in a community of fate irrespective of its internal differences'.[108]

The years of the Great Depression, bringing with them challenges to Britain's industrial monopoly, witnessed the emergence of the 'new unionism' and the re-emergence of socialism, eventually giving rise to the modern British labour movement in its characteristic forms. Its principal novelty consisted in 'substituting socialisation for democratisation as the main political device for the emancipation of the working class'.[109] Yet while the labour movement was increasingly converted to socialism, in however vague a form, in the last two decades of the nineteenth century, it was predominantly in the reformist mould institutionalised by the Labour Party.

What explained the persistence – the iron grip – of reformism in the British labour movement in the twentieth century? The Leninist concept of a 'labour aristocracy' had been adopted by the communist movement after the First World War not merely to

register the undeniable fact of working-class strati-
fication, but to account for the evolution of labour
movements in moderate ideological and political
directions. Thus, British reformism was allegedly rooted
in the existence of privileged strata of workers (not
to mention party and trade-union functionaries), who
enjoyed the fruits of their country's exploitation of its
empire, formal or informal. Conceding his 'polite nod
towards orthodox phraseology' in texts from the late
1940s and '50s, Hobsbawm denied endorsing this as
an adequate *explanans*.[110] In an article first published
in 1949 and revised in 1963, Hobsbawm retracted his
original hopeful conclusion about the prospects for
displacing reformism and summarised his position on
its matrix and maintenance as follows:

> The roots of British reformism no doubt lie in the history of a century
> of world supremacy, and the creation of a labour aristocracy, or even
> more generally, of an entire working class which drew advantages
> from it. Conversely, the maintenance of the belief that British
> capitalism is a going concern ... is a necessary (but probably not a
> sufficient) condition of its survival. A second ... reason ... is, that the
> British labour movement was formed and moulded at a time when
> the dominant tradition was that of a reforming liberal-radicalism
> whose stamp it still bears. However, the third and perhaps most
> important reason for its survival is general rather than specific.
> It is that, in conditions of stable or flourishing capitalism, and
> of official recognition of labour movements, a reformist party is
> 'natural' because it is the obvious and practical policy. ... Therefore
> the spontaneous slope of the political and social landscape will tend

to make labour movements slip towards reformism, unless they resist it; and even – often – when they do.[111]

The British working class had yoked itself to a pre-Marxist form of labour movement which, quite the reverse of resisting spontaneous tendencies towards reformism, had gone with the grain of them, voluntarily entangling itself in a 'web of conciliation and collaboration' since the 1860s.[112] In such a context, the influence of Marxism, and of the Communist Party when it appeared on the scene, had inevitably been circumscribed, restricted to operating as 'the brains-trust of the movement' with the mission of 'making reformism effectively reformist'.[113] The role of the CPGB, realistically assumed by it when not diverted by external promptings as during the Third Period, had typically consisted in seeking to propel the Labour Party to the left, rather than to supplant it as a mass working-class party with a revolutionary difference.

Such, on Hobsbawm's reckoning, was the balance of forces within the labour movement on the eve of Wilson's successful reconvention of Attlee's post-war electoral coalition of manual workers and professional middle classes, ending 13 years of Conservative government in 1964. Reviewing Ralph Miliband's *Parliamentary Socialism* in 1961, Hobsbawm had asserted that '[t]he literature about social-democratic parties is ... a set of variations on the theme of failure', since their proudest boast – the welfare state – was not the goal they had assigned themselves; indeed, was not exclusively social-democratic. In view of this unrelieved history of failure, Miliband's critique of Labour's leadership over six decades was 'rather too moderate'.[114] Nevertheless, the 'vague general aspiration towards a *new* ... society', professed in Clause 4 of the Labour Party constitution, was 'encapsulated in a massive, disciplined, immovable class consciousness which has hardly a parallel in countries of less old-established working-class tradition'. Consequently, pessimism was unwarranted.[115]

Four years into Labour rule, which had failed to arrest relative economic decline and persisted in subordination to US foreign policy, and Hobsbawm was crucially revising his opinions. Anticipating his subsequent line of argument, *Industry and Empire* registered the electoral stagnation of the Labour Party and the ongoing contraction and transformation of its base – the 'traditional' manual working class – in the 1950s and '60s:

> there was a marked sagging in all the institutions of the traditional separatist working-class world. The secular progress of the Labour Party in national elections stopped in 1951 and did not resume. Trade-union membership stagnated. ... What was perhaps more serious, economic change eroded the very foundations of the working class as traditionally understood, that is the men and women who got their hands dirty at work, mainly in mines, factories, or working with, or around, some kind of engines.[116]

More significant than the quantitative diminution of the manual working class caused by deindustrialisation was the qualitative decline in class consciousness induced by its gradual integration into consumer capitalism. Whilst not tantamount to the *embourgeoisement* diagnosed by academic sociologists, the fact that (as Hobsbawm later put it) '[s]ince the 1950s, for the first time in history, most workers in Britain have been able to live a life worthy of human beings', had initiated a de-radicalisation.[117] A revision of traditional socialist perspectives, seemingly vindicated by the 1930s but just as strikingly contradicted by the '50s and '60s, was on the cards. For as Hobsbawm cautiously phrased the point in 1971, 'it may turn out that British workers can, on the whole, enjoy full employment at a high standard of living for quite a long time without first overthrowing capitalism, a prospect which looked hardly credible forty years ago'.[118]

The end of the post-war boom and onset of global recession in the 1970s, impacting with particular severity on the British economy, appeared to suspend a large question-mark over any such prospect. The decade saw an explosion of workplace conflict often led by figures formed in or close to the CPGB, which reached the peak of its influence in the trade-union movement in these years. Hobsbawm cast a consistently sceptical eye over this development, drawing on Leninist and Gramscian critiques of 'economism' and 'corporatism' to challenge its credentials.[119] Industrial militancy over terms and conditions by rank-and-file activists, quite the reverse of providing an opportunity for political 'generalisation' of economic struggles, could constitute a divisive force in working-class politics. As Hobsbawm wrote in an article on the 1970s, tellingly entitled 'Syndicalism Without Syndicalists?':

> The sectionalism of industrial action imposes great and silent strains on class solidarity ...; for much of the militancy aims to increase inequalities within the working class and much has this effect without the intention. ... the gap between a militant and strong labour movement and an organizationally enfeebled Labour Party, whose political support has long been eroding, is dangerously wide.[120]

For Hobsbawm, local circumstances were symptomatic of the profound disorientation of the western left amid the recurrence of economic crisis. By comparison with the inter-war years, it was doubly disabled. It could neither refer to an alternative social model – a socialist society seeming inoculated against the capitalist business cycle; nor offer a programme of the Keynesian variety for surmounting recession.[121] The left, Hobsbawm wrote in November 1978, 'is groping in semi-darkness. We have no clear perspective on how the crisis can lead to a socialist transformation and, to be honest, no real expectation that it will.'[122]

Six months later, the situation took a decisive – definitive? – turn for the worse, with the election of a Conservative government committed to a neo-liberal project for reversing national decline and reviving the animal spirits of British capitalism. The ensuing decade saw Hobsbawm play what he describes as 'a brief cameo part on the national scene of British politics'

– one he recalls with unwonted, ultimately misplaced self-satisfaction in *Interesting Times*, as a minor but worthy role in 'saving' the Labour Party from the ruination threatened by Bennism.[123] His interventions were collected in 1989 in a book whose title speaks volumes – *Politics for a Rational Left* – where they were advertised as 'a critique of left emotion by left reason'.[124] Firmly located by their author within the tradition of Popular Frontism, and mostly published in *Marxism Today* (whose editorial board Hobsbawm joined in 1979), they encountered dissent across much of the British left (including from 'some old and valued friends and comrades').[125]

The crux of Hobsbawm's argument throughout the 1980s was threefold. First, Thatcherism heralded something much more ominous than traditional Conservatism or even a reanimated class-struggle version of it. It was a novel historical phenomenon, a radical, authoritarian neo-liberalism directed towards a comprehensive revolution in British affairs – a political, social and cultural counter-reformation against the post-war settlement (and more besides). Hence its defeat was the overriding priority for the left. Second, the New Right did not enjoy majority support – there was no Thatcherite consensus – and owed its ascendancy to the divisions between (and within) the opposition parties. Hence some way of uniting the latter was imperative. Third, the split in the anti-Thatcher forces had been provoked and/or reproduced by extremist sectarians in the Labour Party unreconciled to the moderation of political objectives required for an anti-Thatcher electoral agreement on the centre-left. Hence marginalisation of the new Labour left and encouragement of a moderate leadership was a precondition of turning the reactionary tide.

In his 1978 Marx Memorial Lecture, Hobsbawm had underscored the alarming disparity as he saw it between the 'almost entirely *economist* militancy' of the burgeoning industrial struggles of the 1970s and the receding 'political expression of class consciousness, which means, in practice, support for the Labour Party'.[126] The result of the 1979 general election was read as confirmation of his concerns. Initially, the rise of the Bennite left thereafter had been greeted as 'an undoubted and welcome advance'; and in a long interview with Benn published in *Marxism Today* in 1980 (but not included in *Politics for a Rational Left*), Hobsbawm praised it as 'a better Labour left than there has been for a very long time'.[127] When he came to respond to the debate set off by his lecture, in the aftermath of the SDP secession, he was cautioning against '[t]he illusion ... that *organization* can replace politics';[128] that winning the Labour Party for socialism was tantamount to a socialist Labour Party winning.

For by now, with the Iron Lady showing her mettle at home and abroad, the Thatcher government had revealed itself to be 'probably the most reactionary government of Britain this century, and certainly (barring Turkey) the most reactionary government in Europe at the present moment'.[129] In conversation with Benn, Hobsbawm had raised the issue of whether there was 'an analogy' between reactionary governance of the present crisis and fascism in the 1930s.[130] Following the Falklands War in 1982, he referred to Thatcher's mobilisation of a revanchist nationalism 'in a rightwing (I hesitate, but only just, to say semi-fascist) direction'.[131] Several years later, he was confiding to a German social-democrat that 'I don't want to use the word fascism lightly but there really is a danger of a powerful right-wing radicalism capable of weakening the whole labour movement and the whole progressive movement.'[132]

The premises were thus in place for a resuscitated Popular Front, necessitating preservation or, rather, recreation of Labour as a '"people's party" of progressive change'.[133] Involving a 'policy of the long haul' for socialism, this was 'the strategy which reaction fears'.[134] Quite why, given the record of the 1930s, was not immediately apparent. Transparent, on the other hand, was the mutation in the conception of the 'broad democratic alliance' advocated by Hobsbawm's own party as recently as the 1978 edition of *The British Road to Socialism*. It had been presented as a means to the end of 'a new kind of Labour Government', committed to a socialist programme and capable of implementing it.[135] It thus formed the centre-piece of a Eurocommunist 'long-term strategy for socialist revolution in Britain'.[136] By the mid 1980s, despite Hobsbawm's claims to the contrary when confronting critics within and without the CPGB, it had dwindled in his exasperated articulation of it into a predominantly defensive tactic, whose advocacy became shriller and closer to the idiom of the mainstream media after the climacteric of the great miners' strike in 1985.

The passionate conviction underlying this was that defeating Thatcher constituted 'the condition of survival for a decent Britain, and of such chances as exist of advancing to a better society'.[137] The intention was clear. So too, however, were the consequences of Hobsbawm's prestigious support for *Marxism Today*'s campaign against Labourism and the left generally – a meretricious iconoclasm which, at the hands of some its keynote writers, ended up 'painting Adam Smith red'.[138] Invoking *The British Road to Socialism*, Hobsbawm credited *Marxism Today* with making a decisive, specifically communist contribution to the debate over Labour's future.[139] It was thus continuing in the role long allotted the Communist Party. But the difference was obvious: the CPGB (or one wing of it) was now acting as vanguard and brains-trust for pushing Labour not to the left, but to the centre and even right – making Kinnockite revisionism effectively revisionist, as it were. Hobsbawm's own Eurolabourist perspective differed from the full 'New Times' prospectus unveiled by *Marxism Today* at the close of the 1980s.[140] In line with it, however, by way of universal specific for domestic ills he touted 'modernisation', floating signifier with a vengeance – largely vacuous in the 1960s, invariably vicious in the '80s and beyond. By the time 'middle England' re-embraced the people's party in 1997, its underlying logic was patent: alternation without alternatives. The Thatcherite settlement had been endorsed as a precondition of electoral success and immutable template of government policy. The autobiographer is left lamely lamenting: 'We wanted a reformed Labour, not Thatcher in trousers.'[141]

To sum up. For much of his career, Hobsbawm had wanted 'a new kind of Labour government' – a socialist one – allocating the Communist Party an important part in achieving it. In the 1980s he lowered his horizons to a Labour government of the old variety, forgetting that it was precisely the failure of social-democratic administrations in the 1960s and '70s which had shattered the electoral coalitions underpinning them, priming neo-liberalism and spawning Bennism. By the second half of the 1990s, what he got was a Labour government of an inconceivably New, positively neophiliac sort – a conversion of Labour justly vaunted by Thatcher as her greatest achievement, but one aided and abetted by the polemics in *Marxism Today* that helped neuter the Labour left.[142] Re-thinking debouched into *la pensée unique-inique*; reconstruction into liquidation. The Labour Party was not saved. In everything but name (and even then some), it was ruined.

Prefacing *Politics for a Rational Left*, Hobsbawm insisted that:

> Rethinking socialist analysis and the socialist project may certainly lead to major, far-reaching, and ... painful modifications of long-held views.... But it does not, or ought not to, undermine the classical socialist case against capitalism, the classical understanding of the

socialist project, or the Marxist conviction that capitalism is destined to be a passing phase in mankind's long historical development.[143]

Marx, Hobsbawm confidently asserted, would have regarded late twentieth-century developments as 'strengthening the case for the necessary supersession of [the capitalist] system, either by another one – or by a relapse into the ages of darkness'.[144] Half a decade later, with the advent of one capitalist world, darkness, if it had yet to fall, had gathered.

3

ENIGMATIC VARIATIONS

Hobsbawm once remarked that 'the really big questions ... have tended to frighten off the professionals in the [historical] trade, increasingly shackled by the double fetters of primary research and specialised knowledge, i.e. generalised ignorance'.[1] Famously, he has not himself shied away from tackling one of the largest of them all, encapsulated in the title under which his tetralogy on 1789–1991 was released in a Folio Society edition – itself a rare privilege for a Marxist historian – in 2005: *The Making of the Modern World.* Unpremeditated at the outset, an enterprise spanning more than 30 years, Hobsbawm's synthetic history of modernity commenced with *The Age of Revolution* in 1962 and proceeded via *The Age of Capital* in 1975 and *The Age of Empire* in 1987, to culminate in *Age of Extremes* in 1994. The Preface to *The Age of Revolution* introduced a theme on which the forewords to its successor volumes performed variations:

The object of this book is not detailed narrative, but interpretation and what the French call *haute vulgarisation*. Its ideal reader is that theoretical construct, the intelligent and educated citizen, who is not merely curious about the past, but wishes to understand how and why the world has come to be what it is today and whither it is going.[2]

Encompassing ascertainable past and present *and* conjecturable future, the original ambition was thus somewhat akin to Comte's *savoir pour prévoir*;[3] alternatively, in Marxian terms, interpreting the world with a view to changing it.

Ages of Progress

The titles of what, by 1975, had been conceived as a trilogy on the 'long nineteenth century', from the French Revolution to the First World War, were more or less classically Marxist, as was their conception of the substance of it and corresponding periodisation (1789–1848/1848–75/1875–1914). The presiding principles, resumed in the 'Overture' to *The Age of Empire*, were threefold. First, the origins of the modern world could be traced to the 'dual revolution' of the late eighteenth century – the British industrial revolution and the French political revolution – which unleashed what Polanyi called 'the great transformation': the transition to an utterly unprecedented, specifically capitalist variety of human society. Second, that transformation, driven by the contradictory dynamic of industrial capitalism under the political ascendancy of its 'characteristic class' – the bourgeoisie – and the banner of its typical ideology – liberalism – had inexorably expanded out from its northern European birthplace to confront and conquer much of the non-capitalist globe in the second half of the nineteenth century, when history 'became world history'.[4] And third, modern world history – perforce Eurocentric for much of the period (*The Age of Revolution* was sub-titled 'Europe 1789–1848') – revolved, in essence, around the history of the uneven and combined development triggered by the impact of a mode of production which, tendentially at any rate, was global. In Hobsbawm's capsular description, '[e]ssentially the central axis around which I have tried to organize the history of the century is the triumph and transformation of capitalism in the historically specific forms of bourgeois society in its liberal version'.[5] For the zenith of 'bourgeois society in its liberal version' also sounded its death knell, as it succumbed to the 'contradictions inherent in its advance': the quietus to the type of society and civilisation created by middle-class liberalism on the western and eastern fronts in 1914–18.[6]

Yet an undertaking that might thereby appear to pertain to the historiographical genre of 'declinism', whilst it did plot a rise-and-fall, did not construe it as an instance of some cyclical pattern to human history. As had been made abundantly clear at the inception of Hobsbawm's project, notwithstanding the descent into barbarism on the killing fields of the First World War, capitalism had a superior future ahead of it: the socialism (and, ultimately, communism) for which, as Marx had all along insisted, it vouchsafed the preconditions – namely, abolition of the material scarcity that was the mainspring of class society and production of the social agency that could finally put paid to it. As we saw in Chapter 2, in *The Age of Revolution* Hobsbawm had alluded disparagingly to the 'polemical defences' being mounted against what, in intent if not in name, he upheld as 'scientific socialism', heir to the Enlightenment progressivism that rightly regarded human history as 'an ascent, rather than a decline or an undulating movement about a level trend'.[7] Even a quarter-century later, now writing not against the backdrop of *Sputnik* and *Vostok* but in the shadow of Chernobyl, Hobsbawm was still striking a guardedly optimistic note about the prospects for the future. For all that history did not 'guarantee us the right outcome, neither does it guarantee us the wrong one'. 'Is there', he mused in the Conclusion to *The Age of Empire*, 'still room for the greatest of all hopes, that of creating a world in which free men and women, emancipated from fear and material need, will live the good life together in a good society?' His answer? A defiant question: 'Why not?'[8] Indeed,

> In terms of the material improvement of the lot of humanity, not to mention of human understanding and control of nature, the case for seeing the history of the twentieth century as progress is actually rather more compelling than it was for the nineteenth. ... But the reasons why we have got out of the habit of thinking of our history as progress are obvious. For even when twentieth-century progress is most undeniable, prediction suggests not a continued ascent, but the possibility, perhaps even the imminence, of some catastrophe.

... We have been taught by the experience of our century to live in the expectation of apocalypse.[9]

Qua matrix of modern progressivism and rationalism in general, the Enlightenment was irreducible to the ideology of a particular social agent. Nevertheless, it had 'fitted excellently into the scheme of things of a rising middle class'.[10] As the bearers of economic and political liberalism, 'the "conquering bourgeois"' (title of a recent book) represented the main vector of human progress in the nineteenth century; and 'the triumph of a bourgeois-liberal capitalism' provided *The Age of Revolution* with its organising principle,[11] furnishing a premise of the unfolding argument. Underlying it was a notion of 'bourgeois revolution' actually more Marxist than Marxian,[12] but in any event crucial for conceptualising and periodising modern history – and not only (but certainly also) because it was constructed by analogy with the 'proletarian revolution' that was projected to set in train a post-capitalist transformation of the bourgeois settlement. (The proletariat will be to capitalism as the bourgeoisie was to feudalism.) Roughly speaking, it pitted an ascending, conscious bourgeois class subject, formed in the interstices of feudal society and embodying economically progressive capitalist property relations, with a programme for juridico-political arrangements conducive to them, against a reactionary aristocracy rooted in a declining feudalism ruled over by an Absolutist *ancien régime*. Yet the disjunction inherent in Hobsbawm's 'dual revolution' – economic in Britain, political in France – indicated a profound problem with the orthodox Marxist schema. It was wittily identified by an original Marxist reviewer of *The Age of Revolution*:

> we have been rather too much in the habit of referring to the Bourgeois Revolution as though to a firm and fixed historical category. In reality it is more in the nature of a speculation, or theoretical construct, or piece of shorthand; it has affinities variously with the ether, the square root of minus one, and the Abominable Snowman. Apart from those very hybrid affairs in 16th century Holland and 17th century England, there is practically only one tangible example, 1789; and 1789 not only ruled out any imitators, but also cancelled itself out, by damping capitalism down instead of gingering it up.[13]

Hobsbawm's confident assertion that the revolutionary wave initiated by the toppling of the Bourbons in France in 1830 'marks the definitive defeat of aristocratic by bourgeois power in Western Europe' was premature, redolent of a tendency to obscure the wider reality that 'the Age of Revolution was also an Age of Reaction'.[14]

On closer inspection, Kiernan's 'one tangible example' of bourgeois revolution – the French 1789 that functioned as exemplar of the historical species, furnishing the gauge of the normal and the exceptional (incompletion, retardation, delegation, etc.) – itself proved problematic. Precisely in so far as its agrarian settlement hampered capitalist development, rather than facilitating it – a 'gigantic paradox' in terms of Marx's 1859 Preface, given due relief by Hobsbawm[15] – might it not be regarded as bourgeois without being capitalist – just as the English revolution of the seventeenth century could be construed as capitalist without being bourgeois? Furthermore, was the French bourgeoisie a class in-and-for-itself in the stipulated Marxist sense? By 1989, writing on the bicentenary of 14 July in defence of the traditional social interpretation, championed by Lefebvre and Soboul, against revisionist attacks on it, from Cobban to Furet, Hobsbawm was reformulating the problem. For all that the French bourgeoisie was a class conscious of itself as such, 'we have to discover why the French Revolution was a bourgeois revolution even though nobody intended it to be'.[16]

'The ubiquitous bourgeoisie': such was the taunting title of a review of *The Age of Capital* that criticised its endeavour to reconcile Marxist theoretical commitments with the implacable historical record.[17] The charge was more respectfully pressed by a commentator on *The Age of Empire*: 'Many historians no longer believe that the 19th century saw the middle classes triumph. ... For them, there is no need to explain ... why bourgeois civilisation collapsed, for the simple reason that it had never actually conquered in the first place.'[18]

Hobsbawm had actually begun to shift his ground in *The Age of Capital*, equating 'the global triumph of capitalism' post-1848 with 'the era of the triumphant bourgeoisie', while conceding that 'the European bourgeoisie still hesitated to commit itself to public political rule'.[19] No longer the politically 'ruling class' in western Europe depicted by *The Age of Revolution*, the *grande bourgeoisie* of financiers, big industrialists and top civil servants was the economically and ideologically dominant class, which 'exercise[d] ... hegemony, and ... increasingly determined ... policy'.[20] Although not explicitly redefined, 'bourgeois revolution' was thus recast in such a way as to disconnect it from the direct, conscious agency of a class. Reconceived as ushering in the legal, political and ideological framework for the reproduction and extension of capitalist relations of production, it was bourgeois not because it was made *by* the bourgeoisie, but because – where successful – such a 'revolution' eventually resulted in the ascendancy *of* the bourgeoisie, which did not entail its monopoly. Accordingly, Hobsbawm argued elsewhere, deduction of what Arno Mayer termed *The Persistence of the Old Regime* (1981) from the variegated socio-political picture presented by Europe on the eve of August 1914 was fallacious. As amply attested by the example of Britain, 'adaption' by older elites or ruling classes, 'and a consequent symbiosis between, for example, a landed aristocracy and an entrepreneurial bourgeoisie or liberalism and ancient monarchy, was common, and quite compatible with the hegemonic status of "bourgeois" ideas'.[21] At all events, the revolutions of 1848, which '"ought to have been" bourgeois revolutions' directed against *ancien régimes* in the greater part of Europe where these survived, failed. Alarmed by the radical ferment among small producers on its left flank, the bourgeoisie abdicated its historical role and 'ceased to be a revolutionary force'.[22] As a result, the initial dissociation between the terms of the 'dual revolution' crystallised into a 'dualism':

> Political revolution retreated, industrial revolution advanced. Eighteen forty-eight ... was the first and last European revolution in the (almost literal sense). ... It failed, universally, rapidly and ... definitively. Henceforth there was to be no general social revolution of the kind envisaged before 1848 in the 'advanced' countries of the world. The centre of gravity of such social movements, and therefore of twentieth-century socialist and communist regimes, was to be in the marginal and backward regions. ... The sudden, vast and apparently boundless expansion of the world capitalist economy provided political alternatives in the 'advanced' countries. The (British) industrial revolution had swallowed the (French) political revolution.[23]

With the great economic boom of the 1850s, 'politics went into hibernation' in Europe for a quarter of a century.[24] Meanwhile, most of the globe was being integrated into the type of capitalist economy pioneered by Britain and became divided between 'advanced' and 'under-developed' countries, the latter figuring prominently among the 'losers' of *The Age of Capital* ('only the congenital optimist would argue that [the positives] outweighed the negatives of the balance-sheet' for 1848–75). Resistance to European expansion with 'the weapons of progress' itself had yet to emerge.[25] The ranks of the 'winners', on the other hand, were joined by non-European powers – Japan and the USA – which took their place in an 'oligopoly of capitalist-industrial powers, jointly exercising a monopoly over the world', while competing with one another.[26]

The era that dawned with the Great Depression of 1873–96 witnessed a mutation in capitalism and a consequent disorientation of liberalism. In response to economic malaise, capitalism was profoundly transformed: 'combination advanced at the expense of market competition, business corporations at the expense of private firms, big business and large enterprise at the expense of smaller'.[27] The new imperialism of the age was not to be conceived as some automatic reflex of domestic business difficulties.[28] At the same time, however, penetration and partition of hitherto unsubjugated regions, part of an accelerating 'process of globalisation' in these decades, indubitably had an economic dimension in the rivalry of capitalist powers competing for markets.[29] In this sense, the creative-destructive dynamic of the capitalist mode of production remained what it had been in *The Age of Revolution*: 'the impersonal groundswell of history on which the more obvious men and events of our period were borne'.[30]

The most obvious of those events was, of course, the outbreak of the Great War, bringing down the curtain on decades of uninterrupted peace in Europe. For the socialist left it was 'an immediate and double catastrophe'.[31] Officially dedicated to peace and internationalism, it was engulfed by a tidal wave of nationalism that had migrated to the right, and assumed aspects of the racism mobilised in defence of inequality against lesser breeds abroad and lower orders at home. The independent, working-class, socialist organisations of the Second International, shot of anarchism and nominally free of reformism, had been formed when European politics emerged from its hibernation during the Great Depression. Embracing Marxism, they championed a version of Enlightenment progressivism. They were,

> almost by definition, parties devoted to that key concept of the nineteenth century, 'progress'. They stood, especially in their Marxist form, for the inevitable forward march of history towards a better future, whose precise contours might be unclear, but which would certainly see the continued and accelerated triumph of reason and education, science and technology.[32]

Thus, the proletariat (or rather, its class-conscious vanguard) became the heir to 'the old bourgeois belief in science, reason and progress' even as much of the bourgeoisie sold its ideological birthright for a mess of reactionary pottage.

If Hobsbawm's account of the seemingly abrupt alteration in bourgeois ideology, betokening the 'strange death' of liberal western Europe,[33] is less than wholly satisfying, it is perhaps on account of his overestimation of original liberal predominance. Kiernan had remarked on his comparative neglect of the pervasiveness of conservatism, especially in religious forms, in *The Age of Revolution*. Moreover, there, by comparison with liberal and socialist philosophies of progress, ideologies of resistance to it had been adjudged 'hardly deserv[ing] the name of systems of thought'.[34] Yet this involved a rationalist bias that equated significant and effective ideology with 'systems of thought', forgetting that '[b]ad coin often drives out good, not in the monetary field only'.[35] Thus, De Bonald and De Maistre, precisely countering *l'esprit de système* and introducing counter-Enlightenment topoi most influentially developed in Nietzsche's *Lebensphilosophie*, were dismissed as inconsequential because they advanced 'arguments verging on the lunatic'.[36] Such myopic rationalism contradicted a prudent maxim set down by Hobsbawm, in the wake of Pascal, when discussing Romanticism in the arts: 'It is never wise to neglect the heart's reasons which reason knows nothing of.'[37]

In 1842 Lord Palmerston lauded commerce as the vehicle of ongoing material and moral progress, declaring it 'the dispensation of Providence'.[38] As translated by Hobsbawm into the firmly secular terms of the bourgeois dispensation, the long nineteenth century contained the seeds of 'the era of war, revolution and crisis that put an end to it'.[39] Thereafter,

> The economic structures which sustain the twentieth-century world, even when they are capitalist, are no longer those of 'private enterprise' in the sense businessmen would have accepted in 1870. The revolution whose memory dominates the world since the First World War is no longer the French Revolution of 1789. The culture which penetrates it is no longer bourgeois culture as it would have been understood before 1914. The continent which overwhelmingly

constituted its economic, intellectual and military force then, no longer does so now.[40]

'For better or worse,' Hobsbawm concluded, 'the century of the bourgeoisie belongs to history.'[41] Logically enough, if implausibly, the class would not rate so much as a mention in *Age of Extremes*.

In an Epilogue to *The Age of Empire*, Hobsbawm drafted what might have been intended to serve as an outline of *Age of Extremes*, or rather its first two parts. Above all, a sea-change was discernible in the rhythm of world history from 1914, as progress, however discontinuous, gave way to 'a series of seismic upheavals and human cataclysms' in the three decades to 1945.[42] After the Second World War, confronted with the extension and consolidation of the Second World, the First had survived the revolutionary-socialist challenge 'by turning itself into something very different from what it had been in 1914'.[43] As a result, despite a myriad horrors,

> There is ... room for great hopes for, in spite of appearances and prejudices to the contrary, the actual achievement of the twentieth century in material and intellectual progress – hardly in moral and cultural progress – is extraordinarily impressive and quite undeniable.[44]

Based on the results of the second half of the twentieth century to date, cautious optimism about the prospects for the twenty-first was in order. Less than a decade later, painting it black, a very different picture was offered, resumed in the last word of *Age of Extremes*: 'darkness'. The overarching reason for the volte-face is not far to seek: the collapse of 'real socialism' that brought the century to a premature end.

Prometheus's Gift, Pandora's Box

Age of Extremes was widely received as not only *Hobsbawm's* masterpiece,[45] but *a* masterpiece – the commanding historical synthesis on the 'short twentieth century', from the outbreak of the First World War to the dissolution of the Soviet Union. It appeared at a time when ends were nigh, most notoriously in Francis Fukuyama's 'end of history' thesis. As Alex Callinicos has noted, it may in some sense be regarded as an Anti-Fukuyama,[46] conceding the massive defeat inflicted on socialism at the century's close, while denying liberal capitalism a definitive triumph – indeed, construing its victory in the Cold War as verging on the Pyrrhic. *Age of Extremes* early on reproved the Fukuyama thesis as metaphysical speculation, adding to the list of mordant remarks aimed at its author since 1990.[47] For Hobsbawm, Fukuyama was (as he dubbed him elsewhere) 'the Doctor Pangloss of the 1990s',[48] therewith presumably deserving deflation at the hands of a latter-day Voltaire. Hobsbawm's own *fin-de-siècle* verdict on the 'old century', returned in *Age of Extremes*, was at the antipodes of the Panglossian outlook misattributed to Fukuyama. The fact that he has repeatedly felt the need to caricature the latter, rather than take his measure, returning to him as if to an unexorcised spirit,[49] might constitute an initial symptom of the evasion of unwelcome truths.

Be that as it may, within the generally favourable mainstream reception of *Age of Extremes* two critical qualifications stood out. The first, familiar enough on such occasions, might be paraphrased thus: impressive book, shame about the Marxism – inviting the rejoinder that if *Age of Extremes* is the former, it is to some extent on account of the latter. The second was incisively formulated by Tony Judt:

> If the virtues of this book derive from its engaged and personal quality, so do its defects – or rather its defect, for there is really only one, though it takes many forms. Because this is a story of Hobsbawm's own lifetime – a lifetime devoted since youth ... to a single cause – he is understandably inclined to see the main outlines and conflicts of the era much as he saw them when they were unfolding. In particular, the categories right/left, fascist/ Communist, progressive and reactionary seem to be very firmly set, and pretty much as they first presented themselves to Hobsbawm in the Thirties.[50]

In short, a seriously flawed text – vitiated not so much by the generally Marxist orientation of its author as by his specifically communist affiliations, consolidated in his late teens.

Whatever one makes of his treatment of it, Judt touched on the neuralgic point. Conjugating the two lines of criticism, we can illuminate some of the paradoxes of *Age of Extremes* by analysing the way in which a certain Enlightenment Marxism governs its architecture and shapes its argument as regards not only the results of historical communism, but also the prospects for contemporary capitalism. The upshot (to anticipate) is that Hobsbawm's history is neither as straightforwardly Marxist, nor as orthodoxly communist, as critics have maintained. Neither, for that matter, is it quite so anti-Fukuyaman, on an attentive reading of *The End of History and the Last Man* at least, as Hobsbawm himself supposed.

Hobsbawm was perfectly conscious of the problem raised by Judt. In the Preface to *Age of Extremes*, he underlined the difficulty with which he had to grapple. Embarking on an account of the twentieth century would be 'an autobiographical endeavour', in as much as he had 'accumulated views and prejudices about it as a contemporary rather than a scholar'; and not simply an observant contemporary but a 'participant observer'.[51] As we saw in Chapter 1, the key to a lifetime's observation and participation lies in the option exercised by many young Jewish intellectuals in Europe in the 1930s:

> We did not make a commitment against bourgeois society and capitalism, since it patently seemed to be on its last legs. We simply chose *a* future rather than *no* future, which meant revolution. But it meant revolution not in a negative but in a positive sense. The great October revolution and Soviet Russia proved to us that such a new world was possible...[52]

It is the confounding of those expectations – the mingled hopes and fears of capitalist ashes and a socialist phoenix arising from them in the twentieth century – that Hobsbawm had to address in *Age of Extremes*. In so doing, he faced a temptation once again unerringly identified by him – this time in his reflections on the bicentenary of the French Revolution: 'All of us inevitably write out of the history of our own times when we look at the past and, to some extent, fight the battles of today in period costume.'[53] 'Anachronism' and 'provincialism': these were foremost among the vices to be avoided in any historiography worthy of the name. The past, the recent past included, was forever another country.[54]

An initial indication of the difficulty in the case to hand was a certain indeterminacy in the title under which Hobsbawm's book was originally published in the United Kingdom: not *The Age of Extremes* – the definite article was omitted and only added subsequently – but *Age of Extremes*. For by what criteria could the short twentieth century be said to be *the* age of extremes? Then there is the substantive itself, basis of the category of extrem*ism* to which it readily gives rise. In contrast to the titles of the nineteenth-century trilogy, here we are uncomfortably close to the vocabulary that forms the stock-in-trade of commentary on, say, Islam today, the Labour Party (including by Hobsbawm) yesterday: 'moderates' vs. 'extremists'. More significantly, the notion is central to the liberal lexicon of the end-of-ideology theorists of the 1950s and '60s – for example,

Raymond Aron in *The Opium of the Intellectuals* (1955), asserting in terms once indignantly repudiated by Hobsbawm that 'the wars of secular religion are ending'.[55] In *The Age of Revolution*, Hobsbawm, overweeningly confident in the ineluctable progress of ideological secularisation, had pronounced religion a 'recessive' force before Enlightenment and its progeny, liberal and socialist.[56] As if attempting to change straight down from top gear to reverse, in the 1990s he was regularly to depict the twentieth century, born out of the wreckage of Enlightenment programmes in August 1914, as the revenge of the recessive, with the dispensations of rival Providences – communist, fascist, liberal, nationalist – clashing head-on in what *Age of Extremes* almost at once calls 'a century of religious wars'.[57] Thus, with the demise of his own ideology, felled by the 'artillery of commodities', Hobsbawm was susceptible to belated subscription to the 'end of ideology' thesis – a forerunner of the 'end of history' thesis – though more as aspiration than realisation, optative rather than indicative, given the recalcitrance of neo-liberalism.

Adoption and adaptation of the notion of 'wars of religion', secular or otherwise, paradoxically attests to Hobsbawm's enduring commitment to a Marxism of a particular temper when interpreting the past and, albeit – or perhaps precisely because – now shorn of its optimism, prospecting the future. Doctrinal orthodoxy in the communist movement from the mid 1930s, that Marxism at once informs and deforms the take on the century of an author who (so the dust jacket of *Age of Extremes* trumpets) 'believes in reason and science'. In a rejoinder to François Furet's portrayal of the communist experience as a *passé plus qu'imparfait*, Hobsbawm remonstrated that it 'reads like a belated product of the Cold War', whereas 'any history of our time which hopes to survive into the next century must, after 1989, begin by trying to take a tentative step away from the ideological and political battlefields of that era'. In the previous paragraph, however, he had averred that 'myth and counter-myth, illusion and counter-illusion in the twentieth-century wars of (secular) religion, can no more be separated by the historian of our century than the Protestant Reformation and Catholic reactions to it can be by the sixteenth-century historian'.[58] Whatever the cogency of that claim, by the time of his autobiography six years later, half-conceding Judt's point, he was acknowledging that his own attempt at a history of our time 'was written with the passion that belongs to the age of extremes'.[59]

We may begin at the end, with the book's summation of the accumulated ills plaguing humanity on the eve of the third millennium. Remarking that there was 'less reason to feel hopeful about the future' than he had been in *The Age of Empire* in 1987, Hobsbawm wrote:

We live in a world captured, uprooted and transformed by the titanic economic and techno-scientific process of the development of capitalism. ... We know, or at least it is reasonable to suppose, that it cannot go on *ad infinitum*. The future cannot be a continuation of the past, and there are signs ... that we have reached a point of historic crisis. The forces generated by the techno-scientific economy are now great enough to destroy the environment, that is to say, the material foundations of human life. The structures of human societies themselves, including even some of the social foundations of the capitalist economy, are on the point of being destroyed by the erosion of what we have inherited from the human past. Our world risks both explosion and implosion. It must change. ...

If humanity is to have a recognizable future, it cannot be by prolonging the past or the present. If we try to build the third millennium on that basis, we shall fail. And the price of failure, that is to say, the alternative to a changed society, is darkness.[60]

Contra *The Age of Revolution*, not only does history not ascend; not only does it not progress, continuously or discontinuously, if necessary by the 'bad side'. What we are instead presented with is imminent regression – as if, socialism having failed, Rosa Luxemburg's forebodings have been confirmed and the alternative to capitalism is (or is set to be) 'barbarism'. Indeed, in an article of that title which appeared shortly before the release of *Age of Extremes*, Hobsbawm deplored 'the reversal of what we may call the project of the ... Enlightenment, namely the establishment of a *universal* system of ... rules and standards of moral behaviour, embodied in the institutions of states dedicated to the rational progress of humanity'.[61] What, for Fukuyama, was materialising, in however protracted and tortuous a fashion, courtesy of the elimination of capitalism's historic antagonist, was for Hobsbawm being negated, in large part because of the self-same cancellation of socialism in its communist incarnation.

Age of Extremes had originally been conceived as 'a sort of diptych' – two eras within the age – periodising the century as an 'age of catastrophe' from 1914–45 and a 'golden age' thereafter.[62] The events of 1989–91 provoked significant revision of this plan, yielding the tripartite structure of the published work:

First, 'the age of catastrophe' – an era of two cataclysmic world wars with their industrial massacres and genocides, punctuated by the disastrous economic slump of the 1930s, volatilising political and economic liberalism and engendering Bolshevism and fascism.

Second, 'the golden age' from 1945 to circa 1973 – the *trente glorieuses* of capitalism's unparalleled prosperity, transforming the globe more rapidly and comprehensively than at any time in human history; of communism's entrenchment in Eurasia, misfiring in its competition with capitalism but spurring the latter to reform itself, seemingly for the good and certainly for the better; and of the Third World's hopeful inscription on the geopolitical map, with the end of European empires by 'prophylactic decolonisation'[63] or force of arms.

Third, and finally, 'the landslide' of 1973–91 – the lapsing of global capitalism into a chronic crisis of regulation, far exceeding the vagaries of the business cycle, even as it prevailed in the 'great contest' with an exhausted communism which, ideologically at any rate, had held centre-stage for close on half a century; and of a great leap backward in the states of the ex-USSR, parts of eastern Europe and sub-Saharan Africa.

Contrary to Hobsbawm's apparent endorsement of it in *The Age of Revolution*, he now disavowed Marx's 'nineteenth-century optimism' that 'mankind always sets itself only such problems as it can solve'.[64] The interment of historical communism and resurgence of an irrational *laissez-faire, laissez-aller* witnessed, if not triggered, an extremity – the last extremity? – of historical capitalism.

Clearly, then, as Perry Anderson pointed out at the time of publication, the most striking feature of this periodisation is the 'reversal of verdicts' it operates.[65] For Hobsbawm, 1991 did not destroy the 'Evil Empire' and transport humanity into a 'New World Order' of liberal-capitalist cornucopia. On the contrary, its 'consequences', reckoned 'enormous and still not fully calculable', were adjudged 'mainly negative': 'the collapse of one part of the world revealed the malaise of the rest' – 'not a crisis of one form of organising societies, but of all forms'.[66]

So much for the periodisation and overall estimate of the short twentieth century. The composition of Hobsbawm's history corresponds, as Simon Bromley shrewdly noted, to two different principles, which help explain its synthesis and table some of the relevant queries it invites, in as much as there is a latent tension between them.[67] The first, in conformity with the preceding trilogy, is that of the development of an incipiently global capitalism in the twentieth century – a history whose internal dynamics Hobsbawm, declining recourse to the conceptual armoury of Marxist economic theory, disclaimed his ability to explain satisfactorily.[68] The second principle is, of necessity, new: that of the confrontation between capitalism and communism – likewise a global history, with its matrix in the First World War (hence *Age of Extremes*' starting point in 1914 rather than 1917) and its terminus in western victory in the Cold War in 1991. The point is this: in the absence of explanations of the *internal* dynamics of global capitalism – generating slump in the 1930s, boom in the '50s and '60s, stagflation in the '70s, and so on – Hobsbawm resorted to accounting for much of its career in the short twentieth century by reference to developments set in train by an *external* dynamic: its systemic competition with communism.

If the Russian Revolution was the fruit, bitter or sweet according to taste, of 1914, credit for liberal capitalism's survival after its near-death experience in the 1930s and '40s, and its mutation in the broadly Keynesian mould of the 'golden age' – 'a sort of marriage between economic liberalism and social democracy'[69] – could in the main be assigned to the presence and performance of the Soviet Union in world politics. Surveying it after the fall, Hobsbawm discerned few intrinsic merits in historical communism. Indeed, with the benefit of hindsight it was evident that 'the strength of the global socialist challenge to capitalism was that of the weakness of its opponent'.[70] Confined to backward, agrarian zones, it effected or accelerated their 'modernisation', an achievement that 'in this respect' – gilt by association – 'coincided with the capitalist Golden Age'.[71] Hobsbawm thus gravitated towards the position of such 'modernisation' theorists as W. W. Rostow, criticised by him in the past, for whom communism was a 'disease of the transition' to modernity – an ideology and policy of planned industrial revolution in countries where the social and political conditions for viable capitalist development did not obtain.[72] Backward communism had not at any stage represented a realistic alternative to advanced capitalism, Hobsbawm now asserted: 'the tragedy of the October Revolution was precisely that it could only produce its kind of ruthless, brutal, command socialism'.[73] *Non*-capitalist without being *post*-capitalist,[74] such communism was doomed. '[F]ailure', Hobsbawm declared without further ado in *Interesting Times*, 'was built into this enterprise from the start'; 'as I now know, [it] was bound to fail'.[75] Given that a German October was not on the cards in 1918, redemption from the west, on which the Bolshevik Revolution had been predicated, was not in the offing.[76] Still, communism's 'direct and indirect effects' outside its borders were momentous,

> Not least because it proved to be the saviour of liberal capitalism, both by enabling the West to win the Second World War against Hitler's Germany and by providing the incentive for capitalism to reform itself and ... through the Soviet Union's apparent immunity

in the Great Depression, the incentive to abandon the belief in free market orthodoxy.[77]

Hence the 'terrible paradox' of the Soviet era unflinchingly stated in a 1996 lecture to mark the award of the Deutscher Memorial Prize for *Age of Extremes*: 'the Stalin experienced by the Soviet peoples and the Stalin seen as a liberating force outside were the same. And he was the liberator for the ones at least in part because he was the tyrant for the others.'[78]

The great cause of Hobsbawm's lifetime, diminished in its pretensions ever to have mounted a genuine societal challenge to capitalism, was thus retrospectively exonerated via its indirect effects on, and unintended consequences for, capitalism. The USSR's victory in the Second World War salvaged economic and political liberalism, sparking a renaissance of it; its sponsorship of planning pioneered the regulatory instruments of the 'golden age'; its 'threat' stimulated the post-war settlement in the First World and decolonisation of what became the Third; its sheer existence conduced to the stabilisation of geopolitics, albeit in the glacis of the Cold War. No wonder that, in the immediate aftermath of the revolutions in eastern Europe, and manifestly prior to arriving at his judgement of inevitable failure, Hobsbawm could write:

The main effect of 1989 is that capitalism and the rich have, for the time being, stopped being scared. All that made Western democracy worth living for its people – social security, the welfare state, a high and rising income for wage-earners, and its natural consequence, diminution in social inequality and inequality of life-chances – was the result of fear. Fear of the poor, and the largest and best-organized bloc of citizens in industrialized states – the workers; fear of an alternative that really existed and could really spread, notably in the form of Soviet Communism. Fear of the system's own instability.[79]

In *Age of Extremes* Hobsbawm identified the alliance against Nazism between western liberal capitalism and Eurasian communism as 'the hinge of the twentieth century and its decisive moment'.[80] This in turn permitted him in the key fifth chapter, 'Against the Common Enemy', to vindicate the communism of the anti-fascist Popular Fronts and wartime Resistance. Here is to be found what Francis Mulhern has defined as 'the moral centre of gravity' of Hobsbawm's account of the century, because the inter-war right menaced nothing less than 'liberal civilization as such':[81]

as the 1930s advanced it became increasingly clear that more was at issue than the relative balance of power between the nation-states constituting the international ... system. Indeed, the politics of the West – from the USSR through Europe to the Americas – can best be understood, not through the contest of states, but as an international ideological civil war. ... And, as it turned out, the crucial lines in this civil war were not drawn between capitalism as such and communist social revolution, but between ideological families: on the one hand the descendants of the ... Enlightenment and the great revolutions including, obviously, the Russian revolution; on the other, its opponents. In short, the frontier ran not between capitalism and communism, but between what the nineteenth-century would have called 'progress' and 'reaction' – only that these terms were no longer quite apposite.[82]

This is the world Hobsbawm has lost – the one he sought to restore in the debates over Labour's future in the 1980s. And while the collapse of communism – explicable in Marxian terms by the fettering of the productive forces by outmoded relations of production[83] – and the disorientation of social-democracy – attributable to the outflanking of nation-states by globalisation[84] – did not rule out what Hobsbawm vaguely invoked as 'the possibility of other kinds of socialism',[85] he now staked out no firm ground for a future socialism inherent in capitalist societies. 'Socialism' predominantly featured in his analysis as an extra-capitalist force, in the shape of the Soviet Union and international communism.

From Hobsbawm's post-lapsarian perspective, with the ongoing trans-nationalisation of a heedless free-market capitalism the outlook was bleak. Humanity had posed itself problems which, even when and where its guardians were cognisant of them, capitalism could not solve. With the 'apparent failure of all programmes, old and new, for managing or improving the affairs of the human race',[86] the conclusion was inescapable, set down in the 'bird's eye view of the century' that prefaces *Age of Extremes*: 'the old century has not ended well'.[87] Above all, a world that had lost its bearings was one in which human beings had lost theirs:

At the end of this century it has for the first time become possible
to see what a world may be like in which the past, including the past
in the present, has lost its role, in which the old maps and charts
which guided human beings, singly and collectively, through life no
longer represent the landscape through which we move, the sea on
which we sail. In which we do not know where our journey is taking
us, or even ought to take us.[88]

Before such uncharted territory, the historian seemed
inclined to emulate the cartographers of old and inscribe
the legend: *Hic sunt dracones*.

For concomitant or consequence of the vortex of
the global capitalist economy, which eluded control
by politics at the level of nation-states or even via
international coordination, and portended ecological
spoliation, was a 'moral crisis' – a crisis of 'the historic
structures of human relations which modern society
inherited from a pre-industrial and pre-capitalist past,
and which ... had enabled it to function'.[89] Decisive in
this regard was the impact of the 'cultural revolution'
initiated in the 1960s, resulting in the prevalence of
'the values of an absolute a-social individualism'.[90] A
consummate antinomianism – *la règle du je*, as it were
– the libertarian

rejection of [conventions and prohibitions] was not in the name
of some other pattern of ordering society ... but in the name of
the unlimited autonomy of individual desire. It assumed a world of
self-regarding individualism pushed to its limits. Paradoxically the
rebels ... shared the assumptions on which mass consumer society
was built ... The cultural revolution of the later twentieth century

can thus best be understood as the triumph of the individual over society, or rather, the breaking of threads which in the past had woven human beings into social textures.[91]

Severance of the ties between, and within, generations and indeed genders heralded the transition, long foretold by classical sociology, from *Gemeinschaft* to *Gesellschaft*.[92] Economic neo-liberalism and cultural libertarianism imperilled the prospects for a habitable planet, their effects unmitigated by the consolatory proliferation of a vacuous community-speak.[93] Ever a good student of Stalin's *Anarchism or Socialism*, Hobsbawm has more than once reminded his readers that the original antonym of 'socialism' was 'individualism'.[94]

As indicated in Chapter 2, Hobsbawm's treatment of the class of '68 in *Age of Extremes* is generally belittling, where not derogatory. On a global scale,

the student revolt of the late 1960s was the last hurrah of the old world revolution ... And yet this was not the world revolution as the generation of 1917 had understood it, but the dream of something that no longer existed: often enough not much more than the pretence that behaving as though barricades were up would somehow cause them to rise, by sympathetic magic.[95]

In the west, whatever the intentions of the protagonists, it was 'more of a cultural revolution, a rejection of everything in society represented by "middle-class" parental values'.[96] Rejecting Aron's characterisation of 1968 and all that as 'psychodrama', only subsequently to meet it half-way,[97] Hobsbawm was obliged to concede revolting youth a degree of efficacy in forcing Johnson's withdrawal from the White House and de Gaulle's from the Elysée Palace. But retracting his sympathetic contemporaneous reaction to the New Left, in *Interesting Times* Hobsbawm took his tart disapproval of its implication in a licentious counter-culture a stage further:

> What if we were wrong in seeing the rebels of the 1960s as another phase or variant of the left? In that case it was not a botched attempt at one kind of revolution, but the effective ratification of another: the one that abolished traditional politics, and in the end the politics of the traditional left, by the slogan 'the personal is political'. Looking back after thirty-odd years it is easy to see that I misunderstood the historic significance of the 1960s.[98]

Here the convictions of a man of the 'old left' have been sacrificed to a veritable neophobia – eclipsed by what the autobiographer confided to be 'the instincts of a Tory communist, unlike the rebels and revolutionaries drawn to their cause by the dream of total freedom for the individual, a society without rules'.[99]

In an essay published in 1972, Hobsbawm suggested that 'an excessive degree of instability and unpredictability in social relations is particularly disconcerting. In Comtean terms "order" goes with "progress"'.[100] As we finish *Age of Extremes*, with its presentiments of impending catastrophe amid alarm that 'human collective institutions [have] lost control over the collective consequences of human action',[101] it is hard to resist the sense that Comte's 'order and progress' has trumped Marx's 'free association' as Hobsbawm's lodestar. In any event, by the gauge of either goal one thing was in desperately short supply at the start of the twenty-first century. It was all that had remained in the box sent with Pandora by Zeus to counter-balance Prometheus's gift of fire to humanity, once its evils had been released: hope.

In Extremis

By way of response, there are two immediate ironies of Hobsbawm's history that need to be noted. The first concerns his treatment of historical communism in its temporary alliance of convenience, and prolonged contention in principle, with liberal capitalism. In vaunting the coalition of 'progress' contra the 'common enemy' of 'reaction' in Part 1, Chapter 5, he glides over something he only deals with at any length in Part 2 (in Chapter 8 on the Cold War) – namely, the Stalinist character of the Communist Party to the alliance, then at the pitch of *its* barbarity domestically, as the great terror followed hard on the heels of forced collectivisation and breakneck industrialisation. It is not that he ignored, let alone exculpated, it. (Just prior to drawing the dividing-lines in the 'international ideological civil war' of the 1930s, he acknowledged that 'the Stalinist tyranny was at that time ... at its worst'.)[102] But if Hobsbawm was justified in his vehement rejection of Krzysztof Pomian's reading of *Age of Extremes* as a pro-Soviet apologia,[103] it is nothing less than the plain truth that the USSR was credited by it with a positive role in world affairs up to 1939 and again from 1941–45. The problem is one of emphasis. Hobsbawm's amalgamation of liberal capitalism and communism into a single party of Enlightenment, casting Joe and Sam as avuncular affinities in a posthumous rehabilitation of Browderism, accentuates the positive at the price of downplaying the negative: the degeneration of communism into barbarism, unredeemed by the thwarting of Barbarossa, which was decisive in besmirching the reputation of socialism in the west (not to mention the east) during the Cold War.

Second irony: at first blush it is counter-intuitive to find the Cold War – era of numerous sanguinary hot wars and other episodes of plentiful bloodletting in the Third World – featuring in Hobsbawm's 'golden age', on the basis that it provided a stabilising structure for the international system. With its termination, Hobsbawm wrote, '[t]he Short Twentieth Century ended in problems for which nobody had, or even claimed to have, solutions ... for the first time in two centuries, the world of the 1990s entirely lacked any international system or structure'.[104] Even were we to grant the substance of this claim, an obvious riposte is that with the 'solutions' on offer during the Cold War, humanity – and especially the wretched of the earth – had its fair share of problems.

Now discounting the understandable 'expectation of apocalypse' he had foregrounded in the Epilogue to

The Age of Empire, and was to reinstate in *Interesting Times*,[105] Hobsbawm portrayed the Cold War as 'a contest of nightmares',[106] whose military component did not tarnish the 'golden age' because it had rarely, if ever, threatened a nuclear conflagration. In retrospect, it was to be regarded as 'a war of unequals' that had (as he claimed elsewhere) 'been waged by one side as a crusade, a cold war of religion, with a brief intermission for confronting the more real dangers of the Berlin-Tokyo axis'.[107] Stalin's post-war preference had been for 'a long-term coexistence, or rather symbiosis, of capitalist and communist systems' – witness the winding-up of the Comintern and (something unimaginable without his instigation or *placet*) Earl Browder's dissolution of the CPUSA.[108] When, following a second wave of revolutions, that proved infeasible, the Soviet Union's stance was – and remained – essentially defensive. If confrontation between American and Russian super-powers had been translated 'from the realm of reason to that of emotion', the principal responsibility was firmly laid by Hobsbawm at the door of the former – likewise an ideocracy, contrariwise a democracy, where crusading anti-communism loomed large in presidential platforms (e.g., Kennedy's in 1960, Reagan's two decades later).[109] Despite escalation of the arms race – tersely dubbed a 'descent into lunacy'[110] – by the 1980s configuration of geopolitics as a competition between antagonist socio-economic systems superintended by rival super-powers increasingly diverged from reality, possessing 'as little relevance to international politics as the Crusades'.[111] Apprised of his own side's *folie* without the *grandeur* in its suicidal pursuit of military parity with the USA, the scene was set for Gorbachev:

> The Cold War ended when one or both the superpowers recognized the sinister absurdity of the nuclear arms race, and when one or both sides accepted the other's sincerity in wishing to end it. ... That is why the world owes so enormous a debt to Mikhail Gorbachev, who not only took this initiative but succeeded, single-handed, in convincing the US government and others in the West that he meant what he said.[112]

Hobsbawm's retrospective devaluation of the systemic antagonism between First and Second Worlds as fundamentally irrational, so much ideological sound and fury signifying nothing in its ultimate stages at least – and thus fit for dissolution by rational presidential agency – is scarcely convincing. The reiterated 'one or both' in the passage attenuates the truth that it was unequivocally one – and for the simple reason that it was the one which had just as unambiguously lost. 'What', Hobsbawm asked in his autobiography, 'did old communists and the general left expect from the USSR in the 1980s except that it should be a counterweight to the USA and by its very existence frighten the rich and the rulers of the world into taking some notice of the needs of the poor? Nothing, any longer.'[113] The exceptions to nothing might strike more than one reader as quite something, and were rooted in the *non*-capitalist character of the Soviet system at home and its – albeit infinitely cautious – *anti*-capitalist systemic logic abroad. Meanwhile, back in the USSR itself, Gorbymania was of course conspicuous by its absence, for as Hobsbawm had noted in the aftermath of the coup against him in 1991, 'his countrymen saw [in their President] only a man who destroyed a clumsy but operational economy and replaced it by a void'.[114] Rudderless glasnost combined with reckless perestroika had yielded the 'slow-motion catastrophe' that was sundown on the Union.[115]

If Hobsbawm was tempted to extend to Gorbachev, quintessential innocent abroad, a version of his verdict on Stalin – crudely put, negative internally, positive externally – the whole drift of his argument in *Age of Extremes* militated against it. For while the end of the Cold War might have called a welcome halt to the arms race, its profounder significance precisely lay in deletion of socialism from the global map and destruction of the geopolitical 'counterweight' that had compelled the advanced capitalist states to ameliorate social inequality and regulate economic anarchy. In 1992 Hobsbawm dismissed any conception of the Cold War as a zero-sum game, wherein '[i]f Communism has lost, then its antagonist, capitalism, must have won'.[116] Much less cogent, the alternative offered in *Age of Extremes* was to perceive it as a negative-sum game at whose end both sides had lost.

The core issue, then, is Hobsbawm's treatment of capitalism itself, for as Michael Mann pointed out, 'capitalism is the enemy whose victory [Hobsbawm] does not quite understand'[117] – to the extent, indeed, that he refused to award it the palm. The acute crisis of regulation and orientation affecting what was in sight of becoming a genuinely global mode of production since the implosion of the Second World was adduced by Hobsbawm as grounds for contradicting western triumphalism post-1991 – Bush Senior's 'the Cold War is over and we won'; and for gesturing at the continuing relevance of a social-democratic variant of socialism, thereby turning the tables on Fukuyama. In drawing – over-drawing – the contrast between the 'golden age' and the 'landslide', Hobsbawm deployed a concept of economic crisis which, for better or worse, was not specifically Marxist. As Bromley noted, it owed more to Polanyi's *The Great Transformation* (1944) – the depredations of disembedded markets – or Schumpeter's *Capitalism, Socialism and Democracy* (1942) – the self-destructive tendencies of unchecked capitalism – than to Marx's *Capital*.[118] In what Hobsbawm subsequently described as 'my Marxist-Schumpeterian approach',[119] there was a signal difference between the slump of the 1930s and the distempers besetting capitalism and, with it, humanity in the 1990s. The latter crisis was conceived not in terms of the internal contradictions of the capitalist mode of production, but of a fatal volatility consequent upon its transgression of its external limits. Consuming everything in its path, capitalism was self-consuming, as it eroded the non-capitalist sources of its own preservation and reproduction: the Second World, the nation-state, the environment, community, family, civility, and so on. The erosion of non-market forces and resources of market regulation was construed as hastening a potentially terminal crisis of the self-*de*regulating and – if left to its own devices – ultimately suicidal global 'free market economy'.[120] Capitalism had sown the wind; humanity was reaping the whirlwind.

In other words, by the criteria of Hobsbawm's prior assimilation of the history of capitalism until the mid 1970s to what Bromley neatly names the 'progress of reason', the contemporary species was above all culpable of irrationality. The fideist of Enlightenment therewith mislaid at least a moiety of his 'Marxist-Schumpeterian approach', eloquently recalled by Justin Rosenberg:

> much of [Marx's] intellectual energy was devoted to a monumental *critique* of Enlightenment thought, showing why the capitalist society associated with it was an obstacle to the realization of its ideals. For the political freedom of the individual which it proclaimed was inseparable from new 'economic' class relations of domination and exploitation. And the enormous increase in human productive powers which it accomplished, precisely because it was driven by the anarchical competitive logic of the market, was achieved at the cost of forsaking rational direction over the course of social development. The twin forms in which these contradictions found expression were a continuing class struggle and periodic economic crises. And it was in these contradictions peculiar to capitalism as a kind of society, rather than in any broader faith in progress, that Marx anticipated the pressure for socialist transformation.[121]

With the dimming of his faith in progress, consequence and corollary of the release of any pressure for socialist transformation, Hobsbawm was led to equate what, by the standards of the 'golden age', was a marked social regression with intimations of the mortality of human civilisation. It was attributable to an absence of public intervention and regulation in defiance of what, in 1968, Hobsbawm had presumed to define as 'the norm of history, and indeed of reason'.[122] Entering the lists against what Freud once called 'the dragon of unreason', Hobsbawm's rationalism prompts the thought that, had things gone as anticipated at the time of *The Age of Revolution*, the final volume of his tetralogy would have been entitled *The Age of Reason*, definite article and all.

As it was, the resurrection of *laissez-faire* – derangement incarnate – following its burial for four decades by the derelictions of the 1930s, almost beggared belief:

> Those of us who lived through the years of the Great Slump still find it almost impossible to understand how the orthodoxies of the pure free market, then so obviously discredited, once again came to preside over a global period of depression in the 1980s and 1990s, which, once again, they were equally unable to understand.[123]

Predictably enough, its partisans were disparaged as 'secular theologians'; and the crisis decades of the 'landslide' termed 'the age of neoliberal economic theology'.[124] In a gesture at even-handedness, the controversy between Keynesians and neo-liberals was portrayed as 'a war of incompatible ideologies', wherein 'economics in both cases rationalized an ideological commitment, an *a priori* view of human society'.[125]

Lacking the acid tests of the natural sciences, subject as these supposedly were to definitive empirical verification or falsification, in the twentieth century economics had 'flourished as a form of theology – probably, in the Western world, as the most influential branch of secular theology'.[126] Still, there was no doubting the identity of the main theological enemy at the close of the short twentieth century: Polanyi's 'stark utopia', or rather dystopia. Fortunately, Hobsbawm claimed, just as both super-powers had in effect lost the Cold War, so their legitimating ideologies had met with their discomfiture at the hands of late twentieth-century reality, in a common ruin of the contending creeds: 'neo-liberal triumphalism did not survive the world economic setbacks of the early 1990s'.[127] Indeed,

> the counter-utopia to the Soviet one was also demonstrably bankrupt. This was the theological faith in an economy in which resources were allocated *entirely* by the totally unrestricted free market, under conditions of unlimited competition. ... No such purely *laissez-faire* society had ever existed. Unlike the Soviet utopia, fortunately no attempt to institute the ultra-liberal utopia in practice had been made before the 1980s. ... The theories on which the neo-liberal theology were based, while elegant, had little relation to reality.
>
> ... it may well be that the debate which confronted capitalism and socialism as mutually exclusive and polar opposites will be seen by future generations as a relic of the twentieth-century Cold Wars of Religion.[128]

Thus, for all that Hobsbawm identified sizeable impediments to what he tellingly described as 'a return to realism'[129] – the lack of a geopolitical counterweight, actual or imagined, and the runaway process of capitalist globalisation – he penned a premature obituary of neo-liberalism. He therewith neglected the sobering lesson imparted by Polanyi as to 'the last remaining argument of economic liberalism today': 'Its apologists are repeating in endless variations that but for the policies advocated by its critics, liberalism would have delivered the goods; that not the competitive system and the self-regulating market, but interference with that system and interventions with that market are responsible for our ills.'[130] The script for neo-liberal responses to the Asian economic crisis of 1997–98, which found Hobsbawm re-announcing 'the death of neo-liberalism',[131] had been written: *Encore un effort...* For the reality was that neo-liberalism refused to lie down and die at Hobsbawm's (and others') behest, as he was obliged to concede in *Interesting Times*,[132] while still ushering the undead into its coffin, stake (no longer hammer and sickle) in hand.

One thing was for sure on Hobsbawm's reading of the century. As a result of the post-war 'social revolution', the gravedigger of contemporary capitalism would not be the declining western working-class, whose cohesion as a collective agent had been increasingly undermined during the 'golden age' and all but destroyed during the 'landslide': 'Prosperity and privatisation broke up what poverty and collectivity in the public place had welded together.'[133] However seemingly divergent their conclusions and evaluations, the unapologetically Marxist Hobsbawm thus had something in common with the forthrightly anti-Marxist Fukuyama: namely denial of any intrinsic contradictory logic to the capitalist mode of production – one of whose major tendencies for Marx, as Hobsbawm had so rightly argued in *The Age of Revolution*, was the creation of a force internal to it with the capacity to challenge and redirect its logic, the 'collective labourer'. As we have seen, in *Age of Extremes*, by contrast, socialism was enacted by a force external to capitalism: the formerly existing socialism of the Second World that galvanised formerly existing social-democracy in the First.

Of course, there were eminently reasonable grounds for Hobsbawm's pessimism of the intellect on this score. It can be argued that capitalism has dug the grave of the gravedigger appointed in *The Communist Manifesto*, and thereby interred the Enlightenment optimism about historical progress embodied in classical Marxism and inherited by what Hobsbawm now demoted to the status of 'communist utopianism' and – what else? – a 'secular religion'.[134] But his desperate optimism of the will in 'the restoration of public authorities', on which *Age of Extremes* wagered in its closing pages, was unavailing. Taking the 'fate of humanity' into their hands, these were charged with the task of 'non-market allocation of resources or, at least, a ruthless limitation of market allocation', fit to ward off the ecological and social degradation caused by the unbound Prometheus.[135] Not economic growth, but a more just distribution of its fruits, was 'the major problem' – an assertion that invites an obvious response: why, other than for a socialist (or social-democrat), should this be *the* major problem?

In any event, given Hobsbawm's diagnosis of the 'difficulties of democratic politics',[136] there was little or no reason to suppose that the imperative policies would be forthcoming. The perennial 'democratic predicament' – in sum, that while 'of' and 'for' the people, government could not realistically be 'by' it or, indeed, its elected representatives (even assuming they were not swine in clover) – had been sharply exacerbated, even as liberal democracy celebrated its triumphant diffusion from the First World to the erstwhile Second and Third. Elections had turned into 'contests in fiscal perjury'; governments were hostage to the vagaries of a 'public opinion' misshaped by a ubiquitous media (what André Tosel calls 'teletotalitarianism').[137] Into the vacuum created by the decline of class politics – more specifically, working-class politics grounded in mass parties founded on universalist Enlightenment slogans and programmes – had rushed 'identity politics' which, rather than composing differences in a 'common interest', multiplied and accentuated them.[138]

Prefacing *Globalisation, Democracy and Terrorism* in 2007, Hobsbawm described democracy as 'one of the most sacred cows of vulgar Western political discourse': 'More nonsense and meaningless blather is talked in Western political discourse today about [it] ... than about almost any other word or political concept.'[139] But in unsheathing his blade against it, Hobsbawm, unlike the Italian Marxist Luciano Canfora (not to mention the author of *The Age of Capital*), takes aim at its purported inefficacy rather than its demonstrable inequality. The main complaint lodged in *Age of Extremes* is not, as one might expect, that formal liberal democracy is substantive capitalist oligarchy – the rule of property-owning elites, eviscerated of any popular self-determination, legitimated by periodic plebiscites – but that it is ineffective, because public authorities are in thrall to fickle electorates, rendering societies unmanageable.[140] The Marxist anatomy of 'bourgeois democracy' had disappeared with the waning of Hobsbawm's faith in any prospect of a socialist democracy, borne by the working-class movement, superseding it and realising the ideal of political freedom frustrated by capitalism.

The late Chris Harman wrote that '[t]he working class is the great missing link throughout Hobsbawm's book'.[141] More generally, as Mann observed, the dramatis personae of *Age of Extremes* differ significantly from those of the preceding trilogy, as classes in general bow out before other social agencies and processes.[142] Hobsbawm's survey of the 'social revolution' did discuss workers in the company of peasants, students and women, whose ongoing emancipation, largely falling within the 'landslide', was elsewhere pronounced 'one of the great historical events of the twentieth century'.[143] Excluded from it, however, was the class alleged by Landes to have been 'ubiquitous' – misleadingly so – in

The Age of Capital. Hobsbawm's unstated rationale had no doubt been provided as far back as 1971, when he claimed that 'the development of capitalism has left its former carrier, the bourgeoisie, behind ... even in its ordinary business operations it finds ... the class which carried it, the classical bourgeoisie, unnecessary'.[144] The adjective is key here. For the superannuation of the '*classical* bourgeoisie' delineated by Hobsbawm at various points in his trilogy did not warrant exclusion of *any* bourgeoisie from the sequel. Employing Landes's term, whether fortuitously or not, Anderson objected that:

> Never since the Gilded Age have financial buccaneers and individual magnates stalked the earth with such giant strides, trampling over labour and swaggering through culture, from heights of power and wealth Gould or Morgan could scarcely have imagined. A glance at press or television is reminder enough of the ubiquity of this tribe. Omitting it, *Age of Extremes* offers a decapitated portrait of contemporary society.[145]

Anderson related this omission from the cast of *Age of Extremes* to a 'spatial anomaly' of Hobsbawm's history of a century that has, after all, regularly been dubbed 'American', contrasting the concentrated attention paid to the USSR with the more dispersed reflections on the USA.[146] Antipathy to what Hobsbawm disdained as the 'USA's pattern of individualist anarchism' may help explain,[147] but does not excuse, this. For in conjunction with intermittent allusions to the decline of US hegemony,[148] it impaired Hobsbawm's ability to see why the end of the Cold War might widely be greeted, not least in the Land of the Free itself, as the dawn of another 'American Century'.[149]

More forgivable at the time of writing was Hobsbawm's failure to appreciate quite how tall China had stood up since embarking on the 'four modernisations' after 1978. To be sure, assigned to the category of 'new and rapid industrializers', China's economy was credited with posting 'spectacular growth' in the early 1990s, such that it was 'the most dynamic and rapidly growing economy of the globe'[150] – a conclusive rebuke to neo-liberalism given its communist supervision. Logically, this dictated rescheduling of 'age of catastrophe', 'golden age' and 'landslide' in the case of the world's most populous state, since what Hobsbawm called the 'calvary of the Chinese people' – the 'lunacies', 'murderous absurdities' and 'mass inhumanity' of the Great Leap Forward and the Cultural Revolution[151] – occurred from the late 1950s to the mid '70s. However, that would have fundamentally disrupted a periodisation which, in partial contravention of Hobsbawm's registration of the advent of 'a qualitatively different world' at the century's close,[152] retained the Eurocentric focus of its commencement.

It may be remembered that in his Epilogue to *The Age of Empire* Hobsbawm had pointed to the potential co-existence of progress and regression, recording a discrepancy between humanity's indubitable 'material and intellectual progress' since 1900, on the one hand, and its lack of 'moral and cultural progress', on the other.[153] Reviewing the astonishing advances in the natural sciences in *Age of Extremes*, he concluded that by virtue of them 'the twentieth century will be remembered as an age of human progress and not primarily of human tragedy'.[154] As the third millennium was about to dawn, he went so far as to declare that 'at [the century's] close, the world is better than it was, with a few exceptions'.[155] By the time of his autobiography, 'the most extraordinary and terrible century in human history' formed a fitting epitaph.[156] The right balance, what might be thought of as an authentically Marxian estimate, understandably proved elusive – not least because of the incommensurability of the relevant rubrics (material, intellectual, moral, cultural). In his conversations with Antonio Polito, Hobsbawm at one stage signals the desideratum of such equipoise:

> The growth in human production and in the availability of wealth is enormous, and the greater part of the world population has benefited from it. This is a feature of the twentieth century that has to be taken into account when making an assessment of what has been *both the best and the worst of centuries*. It has killed more people than any other century, but at its close, there are more people living, and living better with greater hopes and opportunities.[157]

If we ask why the kind of appraisal – 'dialectical', for convenience sake – indicated above is missing from the closing pages of *Age of Extremes*, the answer is ready to hand. As we have seen, with the implosion of 'real socialism', and the unleashing of free-market capitalism, Hobsbawm inferred a dearth of any 'programmes ... for managing or improving the affairs of the human race',[158] a lack of any prospective solutions to the world's rapidly worsening problems, against the background of a crying lack of any international regulatory system or structure. A Hobbesian state of nature writ global loomed.

Was the inference justified? Early on in his last chapter, Hobsbawm inquired: 'What ... were the international powers, old or new, at the end of the millennium?', and responded: 'The only state that would have been recognized as a great power, in the sense in which the word had been used in 1914, was the USA. What this meant in practice was quite obscure.'[159] Fleetingly glimpsed, one eminently discernible future was thereafter enshrouded in the gathering gloom. For in practice what was meant by the existence of the USA as the sole surviving great power was scarcely obscure in 1994, even if it became clearer thereafter. A nonplussed Hobsbawm cannot be reproached with failing to divine the precise contours of the US hegemony commended in the 'Project for a New American Century', and anticipated in *Nostromo* by Mr Holroyd, convinced that '[w]e shall be giving the word for everything'. Yet it is reasonable to suppose that ideological antipathy has here got the better of historical sensibility, as if in the spirit of Freud's sometime confession of incomprehension: 'Yes, America is gigantic – a gigantic mistake.' After all, that imperial project contained a programme for managing, and (so far as its protagonists were concerned at any rate) improving, the affairs of the human race – by promoting international capitalism in

maximum accord with national interests and, to that
end, striving for 'full spectrum dominance'. 'In the
beginning all the world was America', Locke famously
wrote. In the unlikely event that the aspiring North
American masters of the universe have their way, it
(not to mention the Moon and Mars) will be in the
end as well. Possibly for the first time, on this score
the BBC World Service proved a surer guide to early
twenty-first century reality than a participant observer
of much twentieth-century history, when in 2004 it
broadcast a series devoted to the global role of the
USA. Its title? What else? – 'The Age of Empire' (*with*
the definite article).

The Sleep of Reason?

Although neglecting the extensive Marxist literature on
contemporary imperialism – Arrighi or Harvey, Wood
or Anderson, Callinicos or Panitch (to look no further
than Anglophone authors) – since 1994 Hobsbawm has
brought the international role of the USA into somewhat
sharper focus. In *The New Century* he notes that it is
'the only country in history that has been in a position to
claim world hegemony',[160] while expressing incredulity
at the likelihood of its succeeding and dismay at the
results of the endeavour to date. Castigating 'the sheer
effrontery of presenting the establishment of a US global
empire as the defensive reaction of a civilisation about
to be overrun by nameless barbarian horrors unless it

destroys "international terrorism"', Hobsbawm wrote
in a powerful coda to *Interesting Times*:

> September 11 proved that we all live in a world with a single global
> hyperpower that has finally decided that, since the end of the USSR,
> there are no short-term limits on its strength and no limits on its
> willingness to use it, although the purposes of using it – except to
> manifest supremacy – are quite unclear. The twentieth century is
> over. The twenty-first opens on twilight and obscurity.[161]

The continuity with *Age of Extremes* – analytical,
evaluative, figurative – is patent. It is maintained in
the texts written between 2000 and 2006 and collected
in *Globalisation, Democracy and Terrorism*, where
the 'imperialism of human rights' is rejected at the
outset.[162] Hobsbawm proceeds to arraign a megalo-
maniacal US unilateralism, which ignores what (in an
unwonted concession to the reigning hypocrisies) he
on one occasion calls 'the international community'[163]
– euphemism for what British judges used to refer to as
the criminal fraternity. The USA is roundly condemned
as the greatest threat to world peace today.[164] Dashing
hopes that 1989–91 meant the end of wars of (secular)
religion, 'religious wars fuelled by secular ideologies
[have been] reinforced with, or replaced by, a return
to various brands of crusading and counter-crusad-
ing religious fundamentalism'.[165] For Hobsbawm the
'war on terror' is a paradoxical symptom of relative
American decline – a *bellum unium contra omnes*
launched by the Bush administration to shore up the
faltering economic position that belies uncontested

military superiority. Would the USA eventually learn to emulate British realism about the limits of empire? Or 'will it be tempted to maintain an eroding global position by relying on politico-military force, and in so doing promote not global order but disorder, not global peace but conflict, not the advance of civilisation but of barbarism?'.[166]

Inclined, with a Republican still in the White House, to suspect the latter, Hobsbawm scorned 'the neo-conservative and neo-liberal utopians of a world of western values spread by market growth and military interventions'.[167] Consternation at the way in which the USA had squandered the spoils of victory in the Cold War – now admitted – accompanied his contempt: 'The policies that have recently prevailed in Washington seem to all outsiders so mad that it is difficult to understand what is really intended.'[168] *All* outsiders? Unless (like Blair and Brown) they are honorary insiders, Havel, Berlusconi *e tutti quanti*, not to mention Kouchner and Ignatieff – later cited by Hobsbawm as champions of B-52 humanitarianism[169] – would be surprised to hear it. More important than that rhetorical flourish is the imputation of insanity to US policy-makers, thrice dubbed 'crazies'[170] – language better suited to the saloon bar than the lecture theatre, whose use suggests that the empire on which the sun never set has been erected into another 'norm of reason' (possibly even of history), this time imperial. Resorting to a terminology all too prevalent in *Age of Extremes*, where it is used of topics as diverse as fascism and Maoism, neo-liberalism and nationalism,[171] Hobsbawm risks entertaining a teratological conception of recent history. In adopting a posture akin to Thomas Mann's Settembrini, 'for ever blowing on his penny pipe of reason' in defiance of assorted Naphtas, Hobsbawm's self-attribution of a privileged rationality cues a Carlylean response: 'Orthodoxy is my doxy, heterodoxy is thy doxy.'

Writing in 2003, Ellen Meiksins Wood insisted on the intelligibility of the 'war on terror', despite its apparent irrationality. If there was madness in the method, there was method in the madness: 'What we are seeing today, as the Bush administration pursues its reckless policies, may be a special kind of madness; but, if so, it is a madness firmly rooted not only in the past half-century of US history, but in the systemic logic of capitalism.'[172] With his tendency to indulge selected Democrat Presidents – Roosevelt and Clinton, if not (mercifully) Kennedy[173] – Hobsbawm implicitly inscribed a profound discontinuity in US geopolitics with the incumbency of Bush Junior. The enthusiasm with which he can safely be assumed to have greeted Obama is unlikely to have prepared him for policies that are the continuation of war (Nobel *oblige*) by other means – ministrations, where possible, of 'soft power' and 'multilateralism' as variable means to the identical end.

Such considerations were for the near future, in the new conjuncture that opened after 2007 with the escalation of a credit crunch into a financial crash and then an economic slump. We shall glance at Hobsbawm's reaction to it in the Conclusion. For now, we must record the depth of his disillusion in a socialist future. Although using the notion of globalisation descriptively, over-stating its political impact, Hobsbawm naturally dissented from globalitarianism – what Tosel has aptly named the capitalist 'sociodicy' of its neo-liberal artisans and partisans.[174] In *The New Century* he had confided his belief that the left would 'return to its critical view of capitalism. In the last ten years, it has been frightened to say that capitalism is a moral evil. I think it will start saying it again.'[175] With the punctual emergence of an alter-globalisation movement at Seattle in 1999, Hobsbawm could reflect in the Coda to his autobiography that he was 'not surprised to find myself once again among a generation that distrusts capitalism, though it no longer believes in our alternative to it'.[176]

Age of Extremes had seemed undecided as to the implications of the collapse of historical communism for the future of socialism – at one point claiming that '[t]he failure of Soviet socialism does not reflect on the possibility of other kinds of socialism', thereafter conceding that it 'also undermined the aspirations of non-communist socialism, Marxist or otherwise'.[177] If the second line of argument prevailed, if Hobsbawm no longer had much credence in a socialist alternative to capitalism, it was on account of 'the twin crisis of the Bolshevik/revolutionary and social-democratic branches of the Left'.[178] From this retrospective (disad)vantage-point, it became apparent to Hobsbawm that prior to 1917 (and presumably again after 1991), socialism was either a utopian dream or little more than an agitational slogan, for until the Russian Revolution not even the Socialist Left had really thought about what to do in the event of victory. ... Socialist theory was a critique of capitalist reality rather than a real project for the construction of a different kind of society.[179]

The combativeness displayed in the immediate aftermath of 1989 had evaporated. Back then, in a text entitled 'Out of the Ashes', Hobsbawm had itemised the ecological impact and social effects, moral as well as material, of capitalist development which 'define the socialist agenda of the twenty-first century', affirming that '[t]he future of socialism rests on the fact that the need for it is as great as ever'.[180] A decade later, there was precious little sign of any phoenix amid a heap of ashes. Although dismissing Blair as 'a Thatcher in trousers', Hobsbawm was criticising Lafontaine – the German Finance Minister whose ouster sealed the Americanisation of European social-democracy, a rendition all the more extraordinary for being voluntary – as too left-wing; endorsing French Premier Jospin's distinction, no sooner made than mislaid, between a 'market economy' and a 'market society'; and projecting onto Clinton a left-wing vocation of which he, at any rate, was oblivious.[181]

The rousing injunction with which *Interesting Times* ends – 'let us not disarm. ... Social injustice still needs to be denounced and fought. The world will not get better on its own'[182] – thus rings slightly hollow. For Hobsbawm had undertaken a significant

measure of disarmament in what he called 'unsatis-
factory times'. Its rationale was conveyed in the new
Introduction he wrote to *The Communist Manifesto* on
the 150th anniversary of its publication. The founding
document of communism afforded 'a concise char-
acterization of capitalism at the end of the twentieth
century', vindicating Marx's remarkable anticipation
of its developmental tendencies.[183] At the same time,
however, his deduction from them of communism, with
the proletariat as its bearer, was invalid – *et pour cause*:

> The Manifesto's vision of the historical development of 'bourgeois
> society', including the working class which it generated, did not
> *necessarily* lead to the conclusion that the proletariat would
> overthrow capitalism and, in so doing, open the way to the
> development of communism, because vision and conclusion did
> not derive from the same analysis. The aim of communism, adopted
> before Marx became 'Marxist', was derived not from the analysis
> of the nature and development of capitalism itself but from a
> philosophical – indeed, an eschatological – argument about human
> nature and destiny.[184]

With the failure in the twentieth century of revolutionary
and reformist roads alike, the upshot, unstated here,
was obvious to all but the purblind: a gulf – certainly
unbridged, very possibly unbridgeable – between
the desirability of socialism, on the one hand, and
its accessibility, let alone feasibility, on the other.[185]
Wanting in plausible solutions to intractable problems
of agency, strategy and goal, socialism had to all intents
and purposes reverted to utopianism.

Concluding his Introduction, Hobsbawm remarked that:

> the Manifesto ... is a document which envisaged failure. It hoped that the outcome of capitalist development would be 'a revolutionary reconstitution of society at large' but ... it did not exclude the alternative: 'common ruin'. Many years later, another Marxist rephrased this as the choice between socialism and barbarity. Which of these will prevail is a question which the twenty-first century must be left to answer.[186]

The original Marxian referent of that calamitous eventuality was not so much competing socio-economic systems, capitalist and socialist, as 'contending classes', bourgeois and proletarian. But the point retains all its relevance. And we have seen just how insistent Hobsbawm, taking counsel of his fears, has been on it across two decades: with the elimination of communism, the civilisation of neo-liberal capitalism is not *en rose* but *in extremis*. Yet this (as Anderson spotted in 2002) formed part of one of two 'strategies of consolation' engaged in by Hobsbawm, when contemplating the common ruin of the fraternal enemies that were once communism and social-democracy. Neither strategy, Anderson argued, warranted assent. The notion of a congress of the Enlightenment victors post-1989 was always nugatory – comfort for Candides that immediately turned to ashes with the hypertrophy of free-market fundamentalism propelled by an America enjoying unprecedented paramountcy; and the subsequent clash of fundamentalisms, secular and religious. Woe to the victors and vanquished alike was ultimately no more compelling, indicative of a lack of proportion in assessing the new order arising from the rubble of 'real socialism':

> Neither advanced capitalism nor post-Communism is currently in the pink. But, of course, that does not mean the hegemony of the order created at Malta and Paris is weak or unstable, so long as alternatives to it remain little more than glimmers of phosphorescence in a surrounding darkness. To think otherwise is political self-delusion.[187]

If in the guise of its antonym, the cunning of imperial capitalist reason – more (Fukuyaman) Hegel than (Hobsbawmian) Voltaire – might end up having the last word.

Thus matters stood a little over a decade into the twenty-first century by the chronology of *Age of Extremes*. A few short years later, and the New World Order dominated by the United States was in something approaching shock and awe. The debacles of the *Bellum Americanum* in Iraq and Afghanistan had been compounded by Russia's check to relentless NATO expansion in Georgia. Above all, the synchronised economic crisis regularly forecast by Marxists duly exploded, discrediting the liberalising law and the prophets of the Washington Consensus. Perhaps the historian had been upheld in the only forum that mattered – namely, to mix metaphors, what Trotsky once called the merciless laboratory of history.

CONCLUSION
THE WAYS OF THE WORLD

In *Age of Extremes* Hobsbawm writes: '[w]hat was novel about the [inter-war slump] was that, probably for the first, and so far the only, time in the history of capitalism, its fluctuations seemed to be genuinely system-endangering'.[1] The convulsions that racked the global capitalist economy from 2008 arguably marked the second such occurrence. Meltdown was only averted (and then only narrowly) by a communism *à rebours*, in a massive socialisation of loss that gave the lie to the globalitarian *idée reçue* – not least by Hobsbawm himself – of the emasculation of nation-states. As a result, never has so much been owed by so few to so many.

Confessing to a 'a bit of *Schadenfreude*', Hobsbawm told a radio interviewer in October 2008 that what we were witnessing was 'the greatest crisis of capitalism since the 1930s'.[2] Intellectually, it represented 'the equivalent of the collapse of the Soviet Union' for the neo-liberal right; and a more mixed economy was in the offing as a consequence. On the other hand, in apparent contradiction of this scenario, given that the left was 'virtually absent' from the political scene, in the short term, repeating the lesson of the 1930s, the principal 'beneficiaries [would] be on the right'.[3]

In a spirited newspaper article the following April, Hobsbawm maintained that the current systemic crisis was in some respects actually graver than its predecessor, given the advance of capitalist globalisation and the absence of a great power immune to it. If its duration and severity could not be predicted, it would 'certainly mark the end of the sort of free-market capitalism that captured the world and its governments' from the late 1970s.[4] Therewith the prevalent misconception of modern economies as mutually exclusive opposites – either capitalism or socialism – would fade. '[I]nternational bourgeois anarchism' having proved as bankrupt as central state planning, the future lay with 'mixed economies in which public and private are braided together'. However, making the indicated break with 'the ideology, or rather the theology, of global free-market fundamentalism' – ingested wholesale by New Labour in the UK and the Democratic Party in the USA – would be difficult:

> we underestimate how addicted governments and decision-makers still are to the free-market snorts that have made them feel so good for decades. Have we really got away from the assumption that private profit-making enterprise is always a better, because more efficient, way of doing things? That business organisation and accountancy should be a model even for public service, education and research? That the growing chasm between the super-rich and the rest doesn't matter so long as everybody else (except the minority of the poor) is getting a bit better off? That what a country

needs is under all circumstances maximum economic growth and commercial competitiveness? I don't think so.

The requisite rupture with 'the economic and moral assumptions of the past 30 years' necessitated conversion – reversion – to the conviction that wealth was 'a means and not an end':

> Public decisions aimed at collective social improvement from which all human lives should gain. That is the basis of progressive policy – not maximising economic growth and personal incomes. Nowhere will this be more important than in tackling the greatest problem facing us this century, the environmental crisis. Whatever ideological logo we choose for it, it will mean a major shift away from the free market and towards public action. ... And, given the acuteness of the economic crisis, probably a fairly rapid shift. Time is not on our side.

Eight months on, and Hobsbawm's scepticism about policy-makers kicking the habit of a lifetime, belying his proclamation of 'the end of ... free-market capitalism', would appear well-founded. The return of the repressed showed every sign of being swiftly followed by the repression of the returned. At all events, anti-capitalism – for such, notwithstanding Hobsbawm's brisk indifference to 'ideological logos', was the logic of his argument – was thinner on the ground, low let alone high, than other programmes with powerful constituencies.[5] While Zhou Enlai's *attentisme* ('too soon to tell') is particularly well-advised in this context, the balance of political forces has not thus far been deflected to the left and the intellectual battle-ground is dominated by capitalist medicine-men (and women) prescribing a variety of potions and placebos – liberal-regulatory, neo-liberal deregulatory, populist-protectionist, and so forth. The hourly consolidating consensus, in Britain at least, is not the consummation devoutly wished by Hobsbawm, but the imperative of more or less rapidly and deeply cutting state expenditure: public vices, private benefits... Faced with the serried ranks of economic and political Bourbons who have learned nothing and forgotten nothing, even what Hobsbawm once deemed 'a second-best to socialism' – namely, 'saving capitalism from itself' as per the New Deal[6] – has ceded to business as usual.

Responding in his autobiography to the reproaches of a former *Marxism Today* author subsequently installed in Blair's Downing Street, Hobsbawm maintained that 'if critique is no longer enough, it is more essential than ever'.[7] Although the implied contrast is misleading – since when was critique ever enough? – few on the left would dissent from that sentiment. Or, given the total non-recall of the economists, and at a time when a significant percentage of Scottish school children think Ramsay MacDonald invented the hamburger, from another, asserting 'society's need for historians, who are the professional remembrancers of what their fellow-citizens wish to forget'.[8] In both instances, however, while scarcely a voice crying in the wilderness, Hobsbawm seems engaged in something of a rearguard action against overwhelming odds.

Thus, in his closing remarks at a British Academy conference on Marxist historiography in 2004, in terms with which we are familiar, Hobsbawm urged a 'reconstruction of the front of reason' in history, the 'front of progress' that had made great strides up to the mid 1970s, but which was now on the defensive confronted with 'anti-universalism', political and intellectual.[9] As in the past, historical materialism would be a key component of this coalition, which would concern itself with the 'evolutionary history of humanity' re-tabled by developments in the contemporary natural sciences; and, in so doing, find itself addressing what Hobsbawm has called 'the Marxist *Fragestellung*'.[10] 'Not least of the problems for which this is essential', he averred in conclusion,

is the crucial one which brings us back to the historic evolution of *homo sapiens*. It is the conflict between the forces making for the transformation of *homo sapiens* from Neolithic to Nuclear humanity and the forces for the maintenance of unchanging reproduction and stability in human collectivities or social environments, which, for most of history, have effectively counter-acted them. ... Today this balance has been decisively tilted in one direction, perhaps beyond the ability of humans to understand, almost certainly beyond the ability of human social and political institutions to control. Perhaps Marxist historians, with some practical experience of understanding the unintended and unwanted consequences of human collective projects in the twentieth century, can at least help us understand how this came about.[11]

The continuing relevance of a reformulated historical materialism, directed to accurate interpretation of past and present, but divested of any projection of a better future (as opposed to aspiration to it): thus might be encapsulated the last, disabused lesson of a career spanning more than six decades. Yet that would be to slight the political distinctiveness of an author who 'has not only the interest of scarcity but of incomprehensibility'.[12] To do those characteristics, and the fidelity to a lifetime's engagements they imply, anything approaching justice in conclusion, we shall have to look elsewhere – perhaps to Hobsbawm's address at the funeral of Margot Heinemann, whom (as we saw in Chapter 1) he has credited with 'probably [having had] more influence on me than any other person I have known'.[13] For all the tragedies that had befallen her – their – cause in the twentieth century,

> we did not waste our lives, even though many of us lost their hopes. In the first place we, the communists and what was at the time the only communist state in the world, the USSR, won the most important negative victory of this century. We defeated fascism, which would have won the Second World War but for the USSR and the great national anti-fascist mobilizations of which we were the champions and the pioneers. This was the great achievement of Margot's generation.[14]

Heinemann, Hobsbawm concluded, 'would want to be remembered by ... the cause to which she devoted her life and which, through its ideals and its hopes ... will survive the memory of Stalin and what used to be called "really existing socialism"'.[15] We may return the compliment and observe of Hobsbawm what his friend Christopher Hill once wrote of Milton: even – especially – at the height of his intellectual celebrity and official respectability, he would not want his personal fame to be separated from his good old cause.

NOTES

Preface

1. See, most recently, his obituaries of Kiernan and Saville, *Guardian*, 18 February and 16 June 2009 respectively.
2. 'E. P. Thompson', *Independent*, 30 August 1993.
3. Marisa Gallego, *Eric Hobsbawm y la historia crítica del Siglo XX*, Madrid: Campo de Ideas, 2005.
4. Harvey J. Kaye, 'Eric Hobsbawm on Workers, Peasants, and World History', in *The British Marxist Historians: An Introductory Analysis* (1984), revised edition, Basingstoke: Macmillan, 1995; Perry Anderson, 'The Vanquished Left: Eric Hobsbawm' (2002), reprinted in *Spectrum: From Right to Left in the World of Ideas*, London and New York: Verso, 2005.
5. Eric Hobsbawm, Preface to the US Paperback Edition, *Interesting Times: A Twentieth-Century Life* (2002), New York: The New Press, 2005, p. xi.
6. See, e.g., Tony Judt, 'Eric Hobsbawm and the Romance of Communism' (2003), reprinted in *Reappraisals: Reflections on the Forgotten Twentieth Century*, London: Heinemann, 2008; Niall Ferguson, 'What a swell party it was ... for him', *Sunday Telegraph*, 20 October 2002; and David Pryce-Jones, 'Eric Hobsbawm: Lying to the Credulous', *The New Criterion*, 21, 5, 2003.
7. See Michael Burleigh, 'Globalisation, democracy and terrorism', *The Times*, 15 July 2007.
8. See Martin Kettle, 'MI5 cold-shoulders Hobsbawm request to see his file', *Guardian*, 2 March 2009; Geoffrey Levy, 'Eric Hobsbawm, useful idiot of the chattering classes', *Mail Online*, 3 March 2009; Stephen Glover, 'Why do we honour those who loathe Britain?', *Mail Online*, 7 March 2009.
9. Cf. John Saville, *Memoirs From the Left*, London: Merlin Press, 2002.

10. Gregory Elliott, 'In Extremis: Eric Hobsbawm', in Ends in Sight: Marx/Fukuyama/Hobsbawm/Anderson, London and Ann Arbor: Pluto Press, 2008.
11. 'An Interview with Eric Hobsbawm' (1978–79), conducted by Pat Thane and Liz Lunbeck, reprinted in Henry Abelove et al. (eds), Visions of History, Manchester: Manchester University Press, 1983.
12. See Geoff Eley, A Crooked Line: From Cultural History to the History of Society, Ann Arbor: University of Michigan Press, 2005.
13. Eric Hobsbawm, 'French Communism' (1965), reprinted in Revolutionaries: Contemporary Essays, London: Phoenix, 1994, p. 23.

Chapter 1

1. Pieter Keunemann, 'Eric Hobsbawm: A Cambridge Profile 1939', reprinted in Raphael Samuel and Gareth Stedman Jones (eds), Culture, Ideology and Politics: Essays for Eric Hobsbawm, London: Routledge and Kegan Paul, 1982, p. 366.
2. Eric Hobsbawm, Interesting Times: A Twentieth-Century Life (2002), New York: The New Press, 2005, p. 8.
3. Ibid., pp. 17, 31.
4. Ibid., p. 24. 'I have tried to observe it ever since,' Hobsbawm continues, 'although the strain of doing so is sometimes almost intolerable, in the light of the behaviour of the government of Israel' – that 'small, militarist, culturally disappointing and politically aggressive nation-state which asks for my solidarity on racial grounds'. For a recent expression of the strain, see Hobsbawm's contribution to the symposium 'LRB contributors react to events in Gaza', London Review of Books, 15 January 2009.
5. Interesting Times, p. 44.
6. Ibid., p. 47.
7. Eric Hobsbawm, 'Confronting Defeat: The German Communist Party' (1970), reprinted in Revolutionaries: Contemporary Essays, London: Phoenix, 1994, p. 45.
8. Eric Hobsbawm, 'Intellectuals and the Class Struggle' (1971), reprinted in Revolutionaries, pp. 252–3.
9. Eric Hobsbawm, 'History and Illusion', New Left Review, I/220, 1996, p. 121.

10. *Interesting Times*, pp. 67–8.
11. 'Confronting Defeat', p. 52. The verdict is confirmed by Ben Fowkes, *Communism in Germany under the Weimar Republic*, London and Basingstoke: Macmillan, 1984. For an excellent guide to the twists and turns of Third International policy, see Kevin McDermott and Jeremy Agnew, *The Comintern: A History of International Communism from Lenin to Stalin*, Basingstoke: Macmillan, 1996.
12. See, most recently, Eric Hobsbawm, 'Memories of Weimar', *London Review of Books*, 24 January 2008.
13. *Interesting Times*, pp. 73–4.
14. 'Memories of Weimar'.
15. *Interesting Times*, p. 76.
16. Ibid., p. 80.
17. 'Memories of Weimar'.
18. Keunemann, 'Eric Hobsbawm', p. 366.
19. *Interesting Times*, p. 82.
20. Ibid., pp. 95, 93.
21. Ibid., p. 81.
22. Keunemann, 'Eric Hobsbawm', p. 368.
23. *Interesting Times*, p. 96.
24. Ibid., pp. 96–7. Hobsbawm has written that '[i]ts impact on the generation of Marxists between 1938 and 1956 ... cannot be exaggerated': 'The Fortune of Marx's and Engels's Writings', in Eric Hobsbawm et al. (eds), *The History of Marxism – Vol. 1: Marxism in Marx's Day*, Hassocks: Harvester Press, 1982, p. 341.
25. *Interesting Times*, pp. 98–9.
26. In Annan's recollection, Hobsbawm was 'astonishingly mature, armed cap-a-pie with the Party's interpretation of current politics, as erudite as he was fluent, and equipped to have a view on whatever obscure topic one of his contemporaries might have chosen to write a paper': Noel Annan, *Our Age: The Generation that Made Post-War Britain*, London: Fontana, 1991, pp. 254–5. A subsequent remark reveals a side of Hobsbawm rarely, if ever, on display in his written work: 'His heart was at one with his head. When the left foundered he was harrowed by depression. When its fortunes rose he revelled. (In 1968 he returned from the Left Bank bearing a stone of *pave* uprooted by the students)' (p. 368).
27. *Interesting Times*, p. 102.

28. By way of comparison and contrast, readers are referred to writings by two communist contemporaries of Hobsbawm's at Cambridge – Raymond Williams's novel *Loyalties* (London: Chatto and Windus, 1985) and especially V. G. Kiernan's 'Spies' (in Jane Hindle (ed.), *London Review of Books: An Anthology*, London: Verso, 1996). Kiernan, who knew Guy Burgess at Trinity, defiantly concludes: 'I never saw him again after our exit from Cambridge. He did what he felt it right for him to do; I honour his memory' (p. 204).

29. Eric Hobsbawm, 'Cambridge spy story – or the politics of treason', *New Society*, 8 November 1979, reviewing the book that led to the exposure of Sir Anthony Blunt, Andrew Boyle's *The Climate of Treason*.

30. *Interesting Times*, pp. 110–11.

31. Ibid., p. 111.

32. Ibid., p. 123.

33. Ibid., p. 122. For some sense of that influence, see Eric Hobsbawm, 'Address at the Funeral of Margot Heinemann 19 June 1992', in David Margolies and Maroula Joannou (eds), *Heart of a Heartless World: Essays in Cultural Resistance in Memory of Margot Heinemann*, London and Boulder (Colorado): Pluto Press, 1995.

34. *Interesting Times*, p. 118.

35. Ibid., p. 119.

36. Eric Hobsbawm, 'In defence of the thirties', *Granta*, 15 November 1952, p. 12.

37. *Interesting Times*, p. 119.

38. Cf. Hobsbawm, 'Intellectuals and the Class Struggle', p. 252.

39. Eric Hobsbawm, 'Gli intellettuali e l'antifascismo', in *Storia del marxismo*, Vol. 3, *Il Marxismo nell' eta della Terza Internazionale*, Pt. II, *Dalla crisi del '29 al XX Congresso*, Turin: Einaudi, 1981, p. 477.

40. Ibid., p. 449. Spender's book is cited on p. 459 and also alluded to in 'History and Illusion', p. 123.

41. Kiernan, 'Spies', p. 203.

42. 'Gli intellettuali e l'antifascismo', p. 464.

43. Ibid., p. 463.

44. Georgi Dimitrov, *For the Unity of the Working Class Against Fascism*, London: Red Star Press, 1975, p. 135.

45. Eric Hobsbawm, 'Fifty Years of People's Fronts' (1985), in *Politics for a Rational Left: Political Writings 1977–1988*, London and New York: Verso/*Marxism Today*, 1989, p. 108;

Age of Extremes: The Short Twentieth Century, 1914–1991, London: Michael Joseph, 1994, pp. 147–8.

46. Dimitrov, *For the Unity of the Working Class Against Fascism*, pp. 105–6.

47. Eric Hobsbawm, *Nations and Nationalism Since 1780: Programme, Myth, Reality*, Canto edition, Cambridge: Cambridge University Press, 1991, pp. 145–6; 'Fifty Years of People's Fronts', pp. 107–8.

48. Dimitrov, *For the Unity of the Working Class Against Fascism*, p. 119; *Interesting Times*, p. 218.

49. *Interesting Times*, p. 323.

50. Ibid., pp. 339–41, where Hobsbawm quotes 'Reflections on Anarchism' (1969), reprinted in *Revolutionaries*, p. 84.

51. 'Gli intellettuali e l'antifascismo', p. 485.

52. Eric Hobsbawm, 'The Dark Years of Italian Communism' (1972), reprinted in *Revolutionaries*, p. 34.

53. Hobsbawm, *Age of Extremes*, p. 160; 'War of ideas', *Guardian*, 17 February 2007. Hobsbawm concluded 'Gli intellettuali e l'antifascismo' with the declaration: 'For some [surviving 1930s intellectuals], it is the only part of their political past on which, after fifty years of reflection, they can look back with unqualified satisfaction' (p. 490). For a fine recent synthesis, critical of communism from the Trotskyist left, see Andy Durgan, *The Spanish Civil War*, Basingstoke: Palgrave Macmillan, 2007. And cf. Pierre Vilar, *La Guerre d'Espagne*, Paris: Presses Universitaires de France, 1986 – the work of a French Marxist Hispanist greatly admired by Hobsbawm (see his obituary comment in the *Guardian*, 17 September 2003).

54. Eric Hobsbawm, 'The Spanish Background' (1966), reprinted in *Revolutionaries*, p. 81: 'And so we remember it, especially those of us to whose lives it belongs, as a marvellous dream of what might have been, an epic of heroism, the Iliad of those who were young in the 1930s. But unless we think of revolutions as a series of dreams and epics, the time for analysis must succeed that of heroic memories.'

55. *Interesting Times*, p. 153.

56. Nevertheless, as Hobsbawm wrote in 1969, 'There is something heroic about the British and French communist parties in September 1939. Nationalism, political calculation, even common sense, pulled one way, yet they unhesitatingly chose to put the interests of the international movement

first. ... This is how the socialists of Europe should have acted in 1914 and did not: carrying out the decisions of their International. This is how the communists did act when another world war broke out. It was not their fault that the International should have told them to do something else': 'Problems of Communist History', reprinted in *Revolutionaries*, pp. 5–6.

57. *Interesting Times*, p. 153.
58. Ibid., p. 154. Hobsbawm comments that he has been 'unable to rediscover a copy' of the lost pamphlet. A photocopy was, however, preserved in Raymond Williams's papers: see Dai Smith, *Raymond Williams: A Warrior's Tale*, Cardigan: Parthian, 2008, pp. 105–6. I have not been able to consult a copy and rely on Smith above. For Williams's own memory of it, see Raymond Williams, *Politics and Letters: Interviews with New Left Review*, London: Verso, 1981, pp. 42–3.
59. *Interesting Times*, p. 157.
60. Ibid., p. 162.
61. Eric Hobsbawm, 'The Present as History' (1993), reprinted in *On History* (1997), London: Abacus, 1998, p. 306. In *Age of Extremes* (p. 39), 1940–41 was even more glowingly described as 'a marvellous moment in the history of the British people, or at any rate those who were lucky enough to live through it'.
62. *Interesting Times*, p. 159.
63. Hobsbawm maintains that 'Stalin became the chief victim of its unrealism': ibid., p. 163.
64. Ibid., pp. 156–7.
65. Ibid., pp. 164–5.
66. Ibid., p. 166. Hobsbawm had travelled to French north Africa in 1938 on a Cambridge University study grant: ibid., pp. 41, 366–7.
67. 'An Interview with Eric Hobsbawm' (1978), reprinted in Henry Abelove et al. (eds), *Visions of History*, Manchester: Manchester University Press, 1983, p. 30.
68. *Interesting Times*, p. 168.
69. Ibid., p. 169.
70. Ibid., p. 170. Hobsbawm remarks that a party functionary – Emile Burns – requested him to draft 'a memorandum for their discussions on the economic possibilities of postwar capitalist-communist development'.

71. Quoted in Kevin Morgan, *Harry Pollitt*, Manchester: Manchester University Press, 1993, p. 161.

72. *Interesting Times*, pp. 182, 184. Did Hobsbawm have half a mind on himself when, writing on Maurice Dobb in 1967, he remarked: 'There can be no doubt that his official career suffered from his long association both with Marxism and the Communist Party. ... In any event, the stature and influence of a writer is rarely determined by the eminence of his official positions' ('Maurice Dobb', in C. H. Feinstein (ed.), *Socialism, Capitalism and Economic Growth: Essays Presented to Maurice Dobb*, Cambridge: Cambridge University Press, 1967, pp. 8–9).

73. *Interesting Times*, p. 180.

74. Ibid., p. 184.

75. Ibid., p. 186.

76. Ibid., p. 190.

77. 'On the whole ... I don't feel that I've done what I might for the Party or that I've been advancing in my capacity to do so. My sort of professional work is probably the best I can do, but I'd quite like if possible to have more to do with factory workers. I've considered full-time work, but don't think I'm good enough at organization to take the idea seriously': 'Eric Hobsbawm's Communist Party Autobiography' (1952), *Socialist History*, 24, 2003, p. 18. Asked to name three party members to whom reference could be made, Hobsbawm cited Jack Cohen – the CPGB's pre-war student organiser (see *Interesting Times*, p. 118) – James Klugmann and Rodney Hilton.

78. Eric Hobsbawm, 'The British Communist Party', *Political Quarterly*, XXX, 1, p. 37; my emphasis. With utter implausibility, Hobsbawm concluded by suggesting: 'It is doubtful whether there is more moral pressure on party members to do things than there is in many villages to contribute to the church bazaar' (p. 43).

79. Ibid., p. 42.

80. Eric Hobsbawm, 'The Dialogue on Marxism' (1966), reprinted in *Revolutionaries*, pp. 119, 112–13. Cf. *Interesting Times*, pp. 191–2.

81. For a minor contribution to such literature from Hobsbawm, see his Introduction to Jozsef Revai, *Lukács and Socialist Realism: A Hungarian Literary Controversy*, London: Fore Publications, 1950, where it is asserted that: 'The Marxist

differs from earlier champions of the writer as "architect of human souls" (Stalin) in seeing the re-creation of literature as a consciously and collectively planned piece of work under the leadership of the Communist Party', involving a transition 'from the decadent bourgeois to the new socialist approach to literature' (unpaginated but p. ii). On the *Short Course* as 'the compass of communism', see Paolo Spriano, *Stalin and the European Communists*, trans. Jon Rothschild, London: Verso, 1985, pp. 79–89.

82. 'Eric Hobsbawm's Interesting Times: An Interview with David Howell', *Socialist History*, 24, 2003, p. 6. For the west European Communist Parties as operating *in partibus infidelium*, see Aldo Agosti, *Bandiere rosse. Un profilo storico dei comunismi europei*, Rome: Riuniti, 1999: possibly the best one-volume guide to the subject currently available.

83. 'The enemies of Communism accuse the Communist Party of aiming to introduce Soviet power in Britain and abolish Parliament. This is a slanderous misrepresentation of our policy': CPGB, *The British Road to Socialism*, London, 1951, p. 14.

84. Ibid., p. 22.

85. Eric Hobsbawm, 'The Taming of Parliamentary Democracy in Britain', *The Modern Quarterly*, VI, 4, pp. 333, 339.

86. *Interesting Times*, p. 137.

87. Eric Hobsbawm, 'Intellectuals and Communism' (1964), reprinted in *Revolutionaries*, pp. 27–8.

88. *Interesting Times*, pp. 135, 139.

89. Ibid., p. 133.

90. Eric Hobsbawm, 'The Structure of Capital' (1966), reprinted in *Revolutionaries*, p. 144.

91. *Interesting Times*, pp. 133, 141–3, where Hobsbawm confides: 'There is probably no man for whom I have a greater admiration' (p. 141).

92. E. P. Thompson, 'Outside the Whale' (1960), reprinted in *The Poverty of Theory and Other Essays*, London: Merlin Press, 1978, p. 4.

93. Christopher Hill, Rodney Hilton and Eric Hobsbawm, 'Past and Present: Origins and Early Years', *Past and Present*, 100, 1983, pp. 4–5.

94. The editors, Introduction to *Past and Present*, 1, 1952, pp. ii–iii.

95. Eric Hobsbawm, 'Where are British Historians Going?', *Marxist Quarterly*, 2, 1, 1955, p. 14.

96. Ibid., pp. 25–6.

97. 'An Interview with Eric Hobsbawm', in Abelove et al., *Visions of History*, p. 33. See also Eric Hobsbawm, 'The Historians' Group of the Communist Party', in Maurice Cornforth (ed.), *Rebels and their Causes: Essays in Honour of A. L. Morton*, London: Lawrence and Wishart, 1978, p. 32; 'Agendas for Radical History', *Radical History Review*, 36, 1986, pp. 27–8; and 'Eric Hobsbawm's Interesting Times', pp. 7–8.

98. Eric Hobsbawm, 'British History and the *Annales*: A Note' (1978), reprinted in *On History*, p. 239. For Hobsbawm's relations with Fernand Braudel, see *Interesting Times*, pp. 326–7.

99. *Interesting Times*, p. 288.

100. Ibid., p. 285. See also Eric Hobsbawm, 'Has History Made Progress?' (1979), reprinted in *On History*, p. 84.

101. 'The Historians' Group of the Communist Party', p. 32.

102. See, e.g., Bill Schwarz, '"The People" in History: The Communist Party Historians' Group, 1946–56', in Richard Johnson et al., *Making Histories: Studies in History-Writing and Politics*, London: Hutchinson, 1982.

103. Quoted by Raphael Samuel in 'British Marxist Historians, 1880–1980: Part One', *New Left Review*, I/120, 1980, p. 74.

104. See now David Parker, *Ideology, Absolutism and the English Revolution: Debates of the British Communist Historians, 1940–1956*, London: Lawrence and Wishart, 2008.

105. See especially Christopher Hill, 'The Norman Yoke', in John Saville (ed.), *Democracy and the Labour Movement: Essays in Honour of Dona Torr*, London: Lawrence and Wishart, 1954.

106. George Thomson, Maurice Dobb, Christopher Hill and John Saville, Introduction to *Democracy and the Labour Movement*, p. 8. Torr's *chef d'oeuvre*, *Tom Mann and His Times*, was unfinished at her death. As late as 1992, Hill was lauding her as 'the inspiration of us all': Foreword to Harvey Kaye, *The Education of Desire: Marxists and the Writing of History*, New York and London: Routledge, 1992, p. ix. Hobsbawm seems not to have shared this estimate: see 'Eric Hobsbawm's Interesting Times', p. 8.

107. *Interesting Times*, p. 191.

108. Other titles in the series published by Lawrence and Wishart included Christopher Hill and Edmund Dell (eds), *The Good Old Cause: The English Revolution of 1640–60 – Its Causes, Course and Consequences* (1949) and H. Fagan and R. H. Hilton, *The English Rising of 1381* (1950).

109. See Harvey Kaye, *The British Marxist Historians: An Introductory Analysis*, revised edition, Basingstoke: Macmillan, 1995, p. 220. Hobsbawm credits the great historian of the French Revolution, Georges Lefebvre, with invention of the category and practice of 'history from below' in *The Great Fear* (1932): see, e.g., 'On History from Below' (1985/1988), reprinted in *On History*, pp. 242, 269.

110. Eric Hobsbawm, 'Marx and History' (1984), reprinted in *On History*, p. 221.

111. 'The Historians' Group of the Communist Party', p. 31. See also 'The Dialogue on Marxism', p. 119.

112. Eric Hobsbawm, 'The Crisis of the Seventeenth Century' (1954), reprinted in Trevor Aston (ed.), *Crisis in Europe 1560–1660: Essays from 'Past and Present'*, London: Routledge and Kegan Paul, 1965, p. 53.

113. Ibid., p. 32.

114. Samuel, 'British Marxist Historians', p. 95.

115. Ibid., p. 90; and see K. E. Holme (i.e. Christopher Hill), *The Soviets and Ourselves*, London: George Harrup and Co., 1945.

116. *Interesting Times*, pp. 199, 200.

117. See, for example, Eric Hobsbawm, 'Drang nach Osten: some notes on German revisionism', *New Central European Observer*, 14 May 1949 (signed 'Our German Correspondent'), and 'Unrepentant apologetic', *New Central European Observer*, 4 February 1950.

118. *Interesting Times*, pp. 192–3.

119. Ibid., p. 192. The assertion requires qualification, since Hill had published a book on *Lenin and the Russian Revolution* in 1947. For the refusal to attend, for example, to the work of Deutscher, whose *Stalin* had appeared in 1949, see Eric Hobsbawm, '1956' (interview with Gareth Stedman Jones), *Marxism Today*, November 1986, p. 17.

120. *Interesting Times*, p. 194.

121. Ibid., p. 195. As Hobsbawm crisply put the point three decades earlier, 'the communist intellectual, in opting for the USSR and his party, did so because on balance the good

on his side seemed to outweigh the bad': 'Intellectuals and Communism', p. 27.

122. *Interesting Times*, pp. 205–6.

123. For a sober account of developments in the CPGB, see Willie Thompson, *The Good Old Cause: British Communism 1920–1991*, London: Lawrence and Wishart, 1992, pp. 99–113.

124. *Interesting Times*, p. 204.

125. Ibid., pp. 206–7.

126. See Saville's account in 'The Twentieth Congress and the British Communist Party', *Socialist Register 1976*, London: Merlin Press, 1976.

127. Quoted in *Interesting Times*, p. 425, n. 7 and see ibid., p. 207. The list of signatories, headed by Chimen Abramsky and followed by Hobsbawm, included Dobb, Hill, Hilton and Kiernan.

128. Chimen Abramsky et al., letter to *New Statesman*, 1 December 1956.

129. Eric Hobsbawm, letter to *Daily Worker*, 9 November 1956. For Hobsbawm's considered view of the Hungarian 1956 revolution on its fiftieth anniversary, see 'Could it have been different?', *London Review of Books*, 16 November 2006.

130. Thus, in 'The Historians' Group of the Communist Party', he writes that relations 'were not, on the whole, disrupted' (p. 26); while in '1956', denying any 'period of ... strain and coldness', he remarks: 'At least not as far as I was concerned' (p. 21). The qualifications may be significant.

131. See '1956', p. 21, where Hobsbawm remarks that 'in some sense our souls were saved by the fact that we weren't simply struggling against abuses on our own side, we were also fighting what was an obvious case of British imperialism'.

132. *Interesting Times*, pp. 202, 211.

133. Ibid., p. 216.

134. Eric Hobsbawm, *The New Century: Eric Hobsbawm in Conversation with Antonio Polito* (1999), trans. Allan Cameron, London: Little, Brown, 2000, p. 159.

135. Asked in 2003 about his decision to persist with the CPGB, Hobsbawm confessed that 'the more I get asked this question, the harder it is to answer, because I keep wondering how far my answers are in fact projections back of something which wasn't so': 'Eric Hobsbawm's Interesting Times', p. 9.

136. '1956', pp. 21, 23.

137. Eric Hobsbawm, 'The Emancipation of Mankind' (1987), reprinted in *Politics for a Rational Left*, p. 201: 'I do not want to disown my generation and the generation before me, who devoted their lives to the emancipation of mankind and were often killed for it, sometimes even by their own side. I think it is important that one accepts that this was – this is – a great cause.'
138. *Interesting Times*, p. 218.
139. Eric Hobsbawm, Preface to *Revolutionaries*, p. vii.
140. See Eric Hobsbawm, 'The Future of Marxism in the Social Sciences', *Universities and Left Review*, 1, 1957, and 'Dr. Marx and the Victorian Critics', *New Reasoner*, 1, 1957.
141. 'Some Notes about the ULR from Comrade Eric Hobsbaum [sic]', 10–11 May 1958, quoted in John Callaghan, *Cold War, Crisis and Conflict: The CPGB 1951–68*, London: Lawrence and Wishart, 2003, pp. 22–3, 103–4.
142. Perry Anderson, *In the Tracks of Historical Materialism*, London: New Left Books, 1983, p. 69.
143. Preface to the US Paperback Edition, *Interesting Times*, p. xi.

Chapter 2

1. Eric Hobsbawm, Introduction to 1989 Edition, *The Jazz Scene* (1959), London: Weidenfeld and Nicolson, 1989, p. xx. 'The habitual rock-and-roll fan,' Hobsbawm wrote in 1959, 'unless mentally rather retarded, tended to be between ten and fifteen years of age. Probably the universal appeal of the fashion was due to this infantilism' (p. 62).
2. Eric Hobsbawm, 'Count Basie' (1986), reprinted in *Uncommon People: Resistance, Rebellion and Jazz*, London: Abacus, 1999, p. 364.
3. *The Jazz Scene*, pp. 136, 134–5.
4. Ibid., pp. 253–4, 257.
5. Ibid., p. 242.
6. Francis Newton, 'Beatles and before', *New Statesman*, 8 November 1963. For a more nuanced appreciation of another sixties' icon, see 'Bob Dylan', *New Statesman*, 22 May 1964.
7. Raphael Samuel, 'British Marxist Historians, 1880–1980: Part One', *New Left Review*, I/120, 1980, p. 94.

8. Eric Hobsbawm, '1956' (interview with Gareth Stedman Jones), *Marxism Today*, November 1986, p. 230; my emphasis.
9. Eric Hobsbawm, *Interesting Times: A Twentieth-Century Life* (2002), New York: The New Press, 2005, pp. 346–7.
10. Eric Hobsbawm, *Primitive Rebels: Studies in Archaic Forms of Social Movement in the 19th and 20th Centuries* (1959), 3rd edition, Manchester: Manchester University Press, 1971, pp. 2, 10.
11. Eric Hobsbawm, *Bandits* (1969), 2nd edition, Harmondsworth: Penguin, 1985, p. 125 (see pp. 113–26).
12. *Primitive Rebels*, p. 91.
13. Ibid., p. 124.
14. See ibid., pp. 60–2, from which Hobsbawm quotes in *Interesting Times* (p. 136) to convey 'what made us communists'.
15. *Primitive Rebels*, p. 126.
16. Ibid., p. 145.
17. Eugene D. Genovese, 'The Politics of Class Struggle in the History of Society: An Appraisal of the Work of Eric Hobsbawm', in Pat Thane et al. (eds), *The Power of the Past: Essays for Eric Hobsbawm*, Cambridge and Paris: Cambridge University Press/Editions de la Maison des Sciences de l'Homme, 1984, p. 24.
18. Eric Hobsbawm, *The Age of Capital 1848–1875* (1975), London: Weidenfeld and Nicolson, 1995, pp. 2, 253.
19. Eric Hobsbawm, *The Age of Revolution: Europe 1789–1848* (1962), London: Weidenfeld and Nicolson, 1995, pp. 234–5.
20. Ibid., pp. 244–5. Engels had introduced his exposition of the 'communist world outlook' with the statement that 'in its theoretical form, modern socialism originally appears ostensibly as a more logical extension of the principles laid down by the great French philosophers of the eighteenth century': Frederick Engels, *Anti-Duhring: Herr Eugen Dühring's Revolution in Science*, trans. Emile Burns, Moscow: Progress Publishers, 1977, p. 25.
21. Eric Hobsbawm, Introduction to Karl Marx, *Pre-Capitalist Economic Formations*, trans. Jack Cohen, London: Lawrence and Wishart, 1964, p. 10.
22. Ibid., p. 12.
23. Ibid., pp. 33, 38.

24. See 'The Poverty of Philosophy', in Karl Marx and Frederick Engels, *Collected Works*, Vol. 6, London: Lawrence and Wishart, 1976, p. 174.

25. Fredric Jameson, *Postmodernism, or The Cultural Logic of Late Capitalism*, London: Verso, 1991, p. 47. The text by Marx that best conveys this dialectical appraisal is his 'Speech at the Anniversary of the *People's Paper*' (1856), in Karl Marx and Frederick Engels, *Selected Works*, Vol. 1, Moscow: Progress Publishers, 1977, pp. 500–1.

26. See Karl Marx, *Grundrisse: Foundations of the Critique of Political Economy*, trans. Martin Nicolaus, Harmondsworth: Penguin/New Left Review, 1977, p. 162.

27. Eric Hobsbawm, 'Marx, Engels and Politics' (1978), in Hobsbawm et al. (eds), *The History of Marxism: Vol. 1 – Marxism in Marx's Day*, Hassocks: Harvester Press, 1982, p. 258.

28. Karl Marx, 'The Future Results of the British Rule in India' (1853), in *Surveys from Exile*, Harmondsworth: Penguin/New Left Review, 1977, p. 325.

29. George Thomson et al., Introduction to John Saville (ed.), *Democracy and the Labour Movement: Essays in Honour of Dona Torr*, London: Lawrence and Wishart, 1954, p. 8. Cf. Christopher Hill, 'The Norman Yoke', in *Democracy and the Labour Movement*, p. 66 and *The English Revolution 1640* (1940), 3rd edition, London: Lawrence and Wishart, 1979, p. 5.

30. Eric Hobsbawm, 'Progress in History', *Marxism Today*, February 1962, p. 47.

31. Ibid., p. 46.

32. Ibid., p. 48.

33. Eric Hobsbawm, 'From Feudalism to Capitalism' (1962), reprinted in Rodney Hilton et al., *The Transition from Feudalism to Capitalism*, London: Verso, 1982, p. 164. See also *The Age of Revolution*, p. 181.

34. Eric Hobsbawm, 'History and the "Dark Satanic Mills"' (1958), reprinted in *Labouring Men: Studies in the History of Labour* (1964), London: Weidenfeld and Nicolson, 1976, pp. 106, 116.

35. Ibid., p. 118.

36. Eric Hobsbawm, 'The British Standard of Living 1790–1850' (1957/1963), reprinted in *Labouring Men*, pp. 64, 68.

37. Eric Hobsbawm, 'The Standard of Living Debate: A Postscript', in *Labouring Men*, pp. 122–3. See also *Industry and Empire: From 1750 to the Present Day* (1968), new edition, London: Penguin, 1999, Chapter 4, where Hobsbawm writes of 'the universal discontent of men who felt themselves hungry in a society reeking with wealth, enslaved in a country which prided itself on its freedom, seeking bread and hope, and receiving in return stones and despair' (p. 73).

38. *The Age of Revolution*, p. 159.

39. Eric Hobsbawm and George Rudé, *Captain Swing* (1968), 2nd edition, Harmondsworth: Peregrine, 1985, p. 337, n. 26.

40. Ibid., p. 32.

41. Ibid., pp. 243–4.

42. Ibid., p. 253.

43. Ibid., p. xxv.

44. Ibid., pp. 254, 256.

45. *The Age of Capital*, p. 134.

46. Reviewing it, Hobsbawm had forecast that it would become a 'landmark' in its field, while noting (in terms which did not connote unqualified approval) that '[i]t reflects ... a specific atmosphere – neo-Marxist – and a specific group – the New Left itself': 'Organised orphans', *New Statesman*, 29 November 1963.

47. Eric Hobsbawm, 'In search of people's history', *London Review of Books*, 19 March–1 April 1981.

48. Eric Hobsbawm, 'From Social History to the History of Society' (1970/1972), reprinted in *On History* (1997), London: Abacus, 1998, p. 105.

49. Eric Hobsbawm et al., 'Agendas for Radical History', *Radical History Review*, 36, 1986, p. 29.

50. Eric Hobsbawm, 'Has History Made Progress?' (1979), reprinted in *On History*, p. 84.

51. Eric Hobsbawm, 'Look left', *New Statesman*, 24 September 1976; my emphasis.

52. Eric Hobsbawm, 'Dr. Marx and the Victorian Critics' (1957), reprinted in *Labouring Men*, p. 240.

53. Eric Hobsbawm, 'The Dialogue on Marxism' (1966), reprinted in *Revolutionaries: Contemporary Essays* (1973), London: Phoenix, 1994, pp. 119, 110.

54. See Eric Hobsbawm, Preface to *Marxism in Marx's Day*, p. xv.

55. See Eric Hobsbawm, Preface to *Revolutionaries*, pp. vii–viii.
56. '[W]hat he at any rate considered marxism': Eric Hobsbawm, 'The Structure of Capital' (1966), reprinted in *Revolutionaries*, p. 144.
57. Eric Hobsbawm, 'Karl Korsch' (1968), reprinted in *Revolutionaries*, p. 160.
58. Eric Hobsbawm, 'The Principle of Hope' (1961), reprinted in *Revolutionaries*, pp. 137, 141.
59. Ibid., p. 137.
60. See 'The Structure of Capital'.
61. Eric Hobsbawm, 'What Do Historians Owe to Karl Marx?' (1968), reprinted in *On History*, pp. 196, 200 (where Hobsbawm specifically refers to Althusser).
62. Ibid., pp. 200–1.
63. 'The Structure of Capital', p. 152.
64. 'What Do Historians Owe to Karl Marx?', p. 198.
65. Eric Hobsbawm, 'Marx and History' (1984), reprinted in *On History*, p. 212. Hence the appeal to Hobsbawm of the founding text of Anglophone Analytical Marxism, G. A. Cohen's 'admirable and formidable' *Karl Marx's Theory of History: A Defence* (1978), which reinstated the Preface: 'Points of departure', *New Statesman*, 2 February 1979.
66. 'The Structure of Capital', p. 149; Eric Hobsbawm, *Echoes of the Marseillaise: Two Centuries Look Back on the French Revolution*, London: Verso, 1989, p. 100: 'the gap between abstract high theory and the social reality to which it was supposed to relate, had become almost unbridgeable – except by the spiderwebs of philosophical subtlety that could bear no weights'.
67. 'The Structure of Capital', p. 145; 'The Dialogue on Marxism', p. 116.
68. 'Look left'.
69. Eric Hobsbawm, 'Gramsci and Political Theory', *Marxism Today*, July 1977, p. 206. See also 'The great Gramsci', *New York Review of Books*, 4 April 1974.
70. 'Gramsci and Political Theory', p. 206.
71. *Interesting Times*, pp. 352–3.
72. Eric Hobsbawm, 'The Dark Years of Italian Communism' (1972), reprinted in *Revolutionaries*, pp. 32, 31.
73. This is a constant of Hobsbawm's texts on the British, German, French and Italian CPs in *Revolutionaries* (see, e.g., pp. 13, 16, 22, 44, 54, 86). For its latest appearance,

see Eric Hobsbawm, 'Cadres', *London Review of Books*, 26 April 2007.

74. Eric Hobsbawm, 'Confronting Defeat: The German Communist Party' (1970), reprinted in *Revolutionaries*, p. 54.

75. Eric Hobsbawm, 'Radicalism and Revolution in Britain' (1969), reprinted in *Revolutionaries*, p. 13.

76. See Eric Hobsbawm, 'May 1968' (1969), reprinted in *Revolutionaries*, pp. 240–1.

77. *Echoes of the Marseillaise*, p. 102. Cf. *Interesting Times*, p. 334.

78. *Interesting Times*, p. 359. See also Eric Hobsbawm, 'Splitting Image' (interview with Achille Ochetto), *Marxism Today*, February 1990.

79. 'The great Gramsci'. Cf. Eric Hobsbawm, 'Coup d' Etat' (1968), reprinted in *Revolutionaries*, p. 196: 'the persistence of the apparatus of the fascist era makes the solution of fundamental problems in post-fascist Italy almost impossible'. For an excellent critical account of the PCI, see Tobias Abse, 'Italy: A New Agenda', in Perry Anderson and Patrick Camiller (eds), *Mapping the West European Left*, London and New York: Verso/New Left Review, 1994; and cf. Lucio Magri, *Il Sarto d'Ulm. Una possibile storia del PCI*, Milan: Il Saggiatore, 2009.

80. See *The Italian Road to Socialism: An Interview by Eric Hobsbawm with Giorgio Napolitano of the Italian Communist Party*, trans. John Cammett and Victoria DeGrazia, London: Journeyman Press, 1977, p. 15.

81. For an official presentation of the Eurocommunist manifesto, see PCE leader Santiago Carrillo's *'Eurocommunism' and the State*, trans. Nan Green and A. M. Elliott, London: Lawrence and Wishart, 1977. The most convincing justifications of it were by Fernando Claudin, *Eurocommunism and Socialism*, trans. John Wakeham, London: New Left Books, 1978, and Nicos Poulantzas, *State, Power, Socialism*, trans. Patrick Camiller, London: New Left Books, 1978.

82. *The Italian Road to Socialism*, p. 80.

83. Eric Hobsbawm, 'A special supplement: Chile year one', *New York Review of Books*, 23 September 1971.

84. Eric Hobsbawm, 'The murder of Chile', *New Society*, 20 September 1973.

85. Eric Hobsbawm, '1968 – A Retrospect', *Marxism Today*, May 1978, p. 136. 'Nobody', Hobsbawm wrote, 'can say that had [the Czech experiment] been allowed to proceed, success would have been quick, smooth, or even certain. But there is no reason at all to believe that in one form or another the Czech model of a democratic socialism would not have been viable' (p. 135).

86. Eric Hobsbawm, 'Il marxismo oggi: un bilancio aperto', in Hobsbawm et al. (eds), *Storia del marxismo*, Vol. 4, *Il Marxismo oggi*, Turin: Einaudi, 1982, p. 12. '[T]he removal of the worst excesses of Stalinism', Hobsbawm had written in 1969, 'made it clear that even without purges and labour camps the kind of socialism introduced in the USSR was very far from what most socialists had in mind before 1917': 'Reflections on Anarchism', reprinted in *Revolutionaries*, p. 85.

87. Eric Hobsbawm, 'Cuban prospects', *New Statesman*, 22 October 1960.

88. Eric Hobsbawm, 'The cultural congress of Havana', *The Times Literary Supplement*, 25 January 1968.

89. Eric Hobsbawm, 'A hard man', *New Society*, 4 April 1968: 'To sum up the matter briefly, in the eternal debate which divides the revolutionary left into the orthodox and antinomian, calvinist and anabaptist, jacobin and sansculotte, marxist and bakuninite, Che was firmly on the side of the first and against the second.'

90. See Eric Hobsbawm, 'Vietnam and the Dynamics of Guerrilla War' (1965), reprinted in *Revolutionaries*.

91. Eric Hobsbawm, 'Theory turned sideways', *Black Dwarf*, 1 June 1968.

92. 'May 1968' (1969), p. 234. See also 'Reflections on Anarchism', pp. 86–7, 91.

93. 'The Principle of Hope', p. 136.

94. 'Reflections on Anarchism', p. 90.

95. Eric Hobsbawm, 'Intellectuals and the Class Struggle' (1971), reprinted in *Revolutionaries*, p. 253.

96. Ibid., p. 255.

97. The closing line of Eric Hobsbawm, 'Revolution and Sex' (1969), reprinted in *Revolutionaries*, p. 219.

98. 'Intellectuals and the Class Struggle', pp. 256–7.

99. Cf. 'The German Ideology', in Karl Marx and Frederick Engels, *Collected Works*, Vol. 5, London: Lawrence and Wishart, 1976, p. 49; emphasis in the original.

100. See 'Intellectuals and the Class Struggle', p. 266.

101. Eric Hobsbawm, Preface to *Labouring Men*, p. vii.

102. Eric Hobsbawm, Preface to *Worlds of Labour: Further Studies in the History of Labour*, London: Weidenfeld and Nicolson, 1984, p. x.

103. See, e.g., *Worlds of Labour*, p. 83; *On History*, p. 94; and *Industry and Empire*, p. x.

104. Eric Hobsbawm, 'Labour History and Ideology' (1974), reprinted in *Worlds of Labour*, p. 14.

105. Eric Hobsbawm, 'Should Poor People Organize?' (1977), reprinted in *Worlds of Labour*, pp. 293–4.

106. Eric Hobsbawm, 'Notes on Class Consciousness' (1971), reprinted in *Worlds of Labour*, pp. 28–9.

107. *Industry and Empire*, p. 104.

108. Eric Hobsbawm, 'The Making of the Working Class 1870–1914' (1981), reprinted in *Worlds of Labour*, p. 207 – a text described by its author as 'both a tribute to and a critique of E. P. Thompson's remarkable book' (p. 215).

109. Eric Hobsbawm, New Preface to *Labour's Turning Point 1880–1900* (1948), Hassocks: Harvester Press, 1974, p. iii.

110. Eric Hobsbawm, 'The Aristocracy of Labour Reconsidered' (1978), reprinted in *Worlds of Labour*, p. 249, where Hobsbawm summarises his writings on the subject. Cf. 'The Labour Aristocracy in Nineteenth-Century Britain' (1954), reprinted in *Labouring Men*; 'Lenin and the "Aristocracy of Labour"' (1970), reprinted in *Revolutionaries*; and 'Debating the Labour Aristocracy' (1979), reprinted in *Worlds of Labour*.

111. Eric Hobsbawm, 'Trends in the British Labour Movement since 1850' (1949/1963), reprinted in *Labouring Men*, p. 341.

112. Ibid., p. 336.

113. Ibid., pp. 332–3.

114. Eric Hobsbawm, 'Parliamentary Cretinism?', *New Left Review*, I/12, 1961, p. 64. (It should not be assumed that the title was Hobsbawm's own.)

115. Ibid., p. 65.

116. *Industry and Empire*, p. 269.

117. Eric Hobsbawm, 'The Formation of British Working-Class Culture' (1979), reprinted in *Worlds of Labour*, p. 193. For Hobsbawm's rejection of the *embourgeoisement* thesis, see, e.g., *Industry and Empire*, p. 272, and 'Karl Marx and the British Labour Movement' (1968), reprinted in *Revolutionaries*, p. 97.

118. 'Intellectuals and the Class Struggle', p. 248.

119. In 'Lenin and the "Aristocracy of Labour"' (p. 129), Hobsbawm had identified the critique of 'spontaneity' and 'economism' in *What Is To Be Done?* as 'one of the most fundamental and permanently illuminating contributions of Lenin to marxism'.

120. Eric Hobsbawm, 'The 1970s: Syndicalism Without Syndicalists?' (1979), reprinted in *Worlds of Labour*, p. 281.

121. See Eric Hobsbawm, 'The State of the Left in Western Europe', *Marxism Today*, October 1982, p. 10. In the mid 1970s, Hobsbawm had still been comparatively optimistic on the first score: 'In many respects, whatever their own problems, the socialist economies, however imperfect they may be, do not have the problems which leave the capitalist countries in crisis' (*The Crisis and the Outlook*, London: Birkbeck College Socialist Society, 1975, p. 15).

122. Eric Hobsbawm, 'The new dissent: intellectuals, society and the left', *New Society*, 23 December 1978. See also 'Should Poor People Organize?', pp. 282, 287–8.

123. *Interesting Times*, pp. 263, 268.

124. Eric Hobsbawm, Preface to *Politics for a Rational Left – Political Writings 1977–1978*, London and New York: Verso/ *Marxism Today*, 1989, p. 4.

125. See especially Ralph Miliband, 'The New Revisionism', *New Left Review*, I/150, 1985. Cf., e.g., Norah Carlin and Ian Birchall, 'Kinnock's Favourite Marxist: Eric Hobsbawm and the Working Class', *International Socialism*, 21, 1983 and Ben Fine et al., *Class Politics: An Answer to its Critics*, London, 1984.

126. Eric Hobsbawm, 'The Forward March of Labour Halted?' (1978), reprinted in *Politics for a Rational Left*, pp. 21, 20.

127. Eric Hobsbawm, 'The Verdict of the 1979 Election' (1979), reprinted in *Politics for a Rational Left*, p. 25; 'Tony Benn: An Interview with Eric Hobsbawm' (1980), reprinted in Martin Jacques and Francis Mulhern (eds), *The Forward March of Labour Halted?*, London: Verso/*Marxism Today*,

1981, p. 85. Also excluded from *Politics for a Rational Left* was an interview with Kinnock, by whom Hobsbawm would appear to have been duly underwhelmed: see 'The Face of Labour's Future: Eric Hobsbawm Interviews Neil Kinnock', *Marxism Today*, October 1984.

128. Eric Hobsbawm, 'The Debate on "The Forward March of Labour Halted?"', reprinted in *Politics for a Rational Left*, p. 34.

129. Ibid., p. 29.

130. 'Tony Benn: An Interview with Eric Hobsbawm', p. 76.

131. Eric Hobsbawm, 'Falklands Fallout' (1983), reprinted in *Politics for a Rational Left*, p. 54. This piece was Hobsbawm's contribution to a collection of articles from *Marxism Today*: Stuart Hall and Martin Jacques (eds), *The Politics of Thatcherism*, London: Lawrence and Wishart/ *Marxism Today*, 1983.

132. Eric Hobsbawm, 'The Emancipation of Mankind' (1987), reprinted in *Politics for a Rational Left*, p. 200.

133. 'The Debate on "The Forward March of Labour Halted?"', p. 35.

134. Eric Hobsbawm, 'Fifty Years of People's Fronts' (1986), reprinted in *Politics for a Rational Left*, pp. 112, 116–17.

135. Communist Party of Great Britain, *The British Road to Socialism*, London, 1978, p. 4.

136. Ibid., p. 3.

137. Eric Hobsbawm, 'Labour's Lost Millions' (1983), reprinted in *Politics for a Rational Left*, p. 66.

138. See Preface to *Politics for a Rational Left*, p. 4.

139. See 'The Retreat into Extremism' (1985), reprinted in *Politics for a Rational Left*, pp. 97–8.

140. Significantly, Hobsbawm was not among the writers on this theme and did not contribute to Stuart Hall and Martin Jacques (eds), *New Times: The Changing Face of Politics in the 1990s*, London: Lawrence and Wishart/*Marxism Today*, 1989.

141. *Interesting Times*, p. 276.

142. An excellent account can be found in Leo Panitch and Colin Leys, *The End of Parliamentary Socialism: From New Left to New Labour*, London and New York: Verso, 1997. For my own thoughts on the 1980s and early '90s, see Gregory Elliott, *Labourism and the English Genius: The Strange*

Death of Labour England?, London and New York: Verso, 1993.
143. *Politics for a Rational Left*, p. 4.
144. Ibid., p. 5.

Chapter 3

1. Eric Hobsbawm, 'From Babylon to Manchester', *New Statesman*, 7 February 1975.
2. Eric Hobsbawm, *The Age of Revolution: Europe 1789–1848* (1962), London: Weidenfeld and Nicolson, 1995, p. 11. See also *The Age of Capital 1848–1875* (1975), London: Weidenfeld and Nicolson, 1995, p. xi; *The Age of Empire 1875–1914* (1987), London: Weidenfeld and Nicolson, 1995, pp. xi–xii; and *Age of Extremes: The Short Twentieth Century, 1914–1991*, London: Michael Joseph, 1994, p. xii.
3. Cf. Eric Hobsbawm, 'Looking Forward: History and the Future' (1981), reprinted in *On History* (1997), London: Abacus, 1998, p. 57.
4. *The Age of Capital*, p. 47.
5. *The Age of Empire*, pp. 8–9.
6. Ibid., p. 10.
7. See *The Age of Revolution*, pp. 244–5, 234–5.
8. *The Age of Empire*, p. 340.
9. Ibid., p. 330.
10. *The Age of Revolution*, pp. 21–2, 218.
11. Ibid., pp. 2–3.
12. Hobsbawm has noted that the category occurs no more than a dozen times in the 38 volumes of Marx's and Engels's *Werke*: *Echoes of the Marseillaise: Two Centuries Look Back on the French Revolution*, London: Verso, 1990, p. 7.
13. Victor Kiernan, 'Revolution and Reaction 1789–1848', *New Left Review*, I/19, 1963, p. 74.
14. *The Age of Revolution*, p. 111; Kiernan, 'Revolution and Reaction', p. 73.
15. See *The Age of Revolution*, pp. 177–8; see also pp. 69–70.
16. *Echoes of the Marseillaise*, p. 9. See also 'Marx and History' (1983/1984), reprinted in *On History*, p. 222: 'As Marxists, or indeed realistic observers of history, we will not follow the critics in denying the existence of such revolutions, or in denying that the seventeenth-century English revolutions and the French revolution did mark fundamental changes

and "bourgeois" reorientations of their societies. But we shall have to think more precisely about what we mean.'

17. See David Landes, 'The ubiquitous bourgeoisie', *The Times Literary Supplement*, 4 June 1976.

18. David Cannadine, 'The strange death of liberal Europe', *New Society*, 23 October 1987.

19. *The Age of Capital*, p. 3.

20. Ibid., p. 249; cf. *The Age of Revolution*, p. 140.

21. Eric Hobsbawm, 'Revolution', in Roy Porter and Mikulas Teich (eds), *Revolution in History*, Cambridge: Cambridge University Press, 1986, p. 27: an important text based on a paper given in 1975. Cf. Arno J. Mayer, *The Persistence of the Old Regime: Europe to the Great War*, London: Croom Helm, 1981. For a probing review of *The Age of Capital* that clarifies these (and other) issues, see Gareth Stedman Jones, 'Society and Politics at the Beginning of the World Economy', *Cambridge Journal of Economics*, 1, 1977.

22. *The Age of Capital*, pp. 24, 20.

23. Ibid., pp. 2–3.

24. Ibid., p. 31.

25. Ibid., pp. 133–4. See also *The Age of Revolution*, p. 26: 'The dual revolution was to make European expansion irresistible, though it was also to provide the non-European world with the conditions and equipment for its eventual counter-attack.'

26. *The Age of Capital*, p. 81.

27. *The Age of Empire*, p. 44; and see also pp. 50–5.

28. 'Economic development is not a sort of ventriloquist with the rest of history as its dummy': ibid., p. 61.

29. See, e.g., ibid., pp. 66–7, 72, 76. Some years before it became an *idée reçue* (not to mention *fixe*), 'globalisation' – albeit more as description than explanation, let alone prescription – was a recurrent theme in *The Age of Empire*: see, e.g., pp. 14, 48, 62, 315, 336.

30. *The Age of Revolution*, p. 28.

31. *The Age of Empire*, p. 327.

32. Ibid., p. 138; see also p. 267.

33. See ibid., p. 190, where it is suggested that the title of Dangerfield's celebrated book on 'liberal England' could be extended to western Europe.

34. *The Age of Revolution*, p. 245.

35. Kiernan, 'Revolution and Reaction', p. 75.

36. *The Age of Revolution*, p. 247.

37. Ibid., p. 263. Evoking reactions to the advent of war in 1914, Hobsbawm evinces no little ability to maintain a distinction, drawn elsewhere, between the 'rational' and the 'comprehensible', without sacrificing the reasons of the heart on the altar of Reason *tout court*: 'In a way its coming was widely felt as a release and a relief, especially by the young of the middle classes – men very much more than women … it meant an end to the superficialities and frivolities of bourgeois society, the boring gradualism of nineteenth-century improvement, the tranquillity and peaceful order which was the liberal utopia for the twentieth century. … After a long wait in the auditorium, it meant the opening of the curtain on a great and exciting historical drama in which the audience found itself to be the actors': *The Age of Empire*, p. 326; and see 'On History from Below' (1985/1988), reprinted in *On History*, p. 283.

38. Quoted in *The Age of Revolution*, p. 298.

39. *The Age of Empire*, p. 327.

40. Ibid., p. 11.

41. Ibid., p. 12.

42. Ibid., p. 329; see pp. 329–34.

43. Ibid., p. 332.

44. Ibid., p. 340.

45. See, e.g., Perry Anderson, 'Darkness falls', *Guardian*, 8 November 1994, and Göran Therborn, 'The Autobiography of the Twentieth Century', *New Left Review*, I/214, 1995. Anderson's assessment was reiterated in the lengthy essays devoted to Hobsbawm in the *London Review of Books* in 2002 and reprinted as 'The Vanquished Left: Eric Hobsbawm', in *Spectrum: From Right to Left in the World of Ideas*, London and New York: Verso, 2005.

46. See Alex Callinicos, 'The Drama of Revolution and Reaction: Marxist History and the Twentieth Century', in Chris Wickham (ed.), *Marxist History-writing for the Twenty-first Century*, Oxford: British Academy/Oxford University Press, 2007, p. 170.

47. See *Age of Extremes*, p. 6; see also pp. 9, 420, 459. Cf. Eric Hobsbawm, 'Goodbye to All That' (1990), reprinted in Robin Blackburn (ed.), *After the Fall: The Failure of Communism and the Future of Socialism*, London and New York: Verso, 1991, p. 124, and 'The Crisis of Today's Ideologies', *New Left Review*, I/192, p. 60.

48. Eric Hobsbawm, *The New Century: Eric Hobsbawm in Conversation with Antonio Polito* (1999), trans. Allan Cameron, London: Little, Brown, 2000, p. 166; see also p. 114.

49. See, most recently, Eric Hobsbawm, 'War, Peace and Hegemony at the Beginning of the Twenty-First Century' (2004), in *Globalisation, Democracy and Terrorism*, London: Little, Brown, 2007, p. 31; and for a discussion that refutes Hobsbawm's (and others') misapprehensions, Perry Anderson, 'The Ends of History', in *A Zone of Engagement*, London and New York: Verso, 1992. For my own thoughts, see Gregory Elliott, 'Full Spectrum Dominance? Francis Fukuyama', in *Ends in Sight: Marx/Fukuyama/Hobsbawm/Anderson*, London: Pluto Press, 2008.

50. Tony Judt, 'Downhill all the way', *New York Review of Books*, 25 May 1995.

51. *Age of Extremes*, pp. ix–x.

52. Eric Hobsbawm, 'Intellectuals and the Class Struggle' (1971), reprinted in *Revolutionaries: Contemporary Essays* (1973), London: Phoenix, 1994, pp. 250–1.

53. *Echoes of the Marseillaise*, p. xiv.

54. See, e.g., Eric Hobsbawm, *Interesting Times: A Twentieth-Century Life* (2002), New York: The New Press, 2005, p. 414.

55. Raymond Aron, *The Opium of the Intellectuals*, trans. Terence Kilmartin, London: Secker and Warburg, 1957, p. xviii. Cf. Eric Hobsbawm, 'Intellectuals and Communism' (1964), reprinted in *Revolutionaries*, p. 26.

56. *The Age of Revolution*, p. 220.

57. *Age of Extremes*, p. 5. Seriatim in *Age of Extremes*, the theme recurs in Hobsbawm's writings in the 1990s: see, e.g., *On History*, pp. x, 314, 339, 348.

58. Eric Hobsbawm, 'History and Illusion', *New Left Review*, I/220, 1996, pp. 125, 124. For Furet's history, see *Le Passé d'une illusion. Essai sur l'idée communiste au xxe siècle*, Paris: Robert Laffont, 1995.

59. *Interesting Times*, p. xiii.

60. *Age of Extremes*, pp. 584–5.

61. Eric Hobsbawm, 'Barbarism: A User's Guide' (1994), reprinted in *On History*, p. 335: 'one of the few things that stands between us and an accelerated descent into darkness

is the set of values inherited from the ... Enlightenment'
(p. 336).

62. See Eric Hobsbawm, 'The Present as History' (1993),
    reprinted in *On History*, p. 312.

63. *Age of Extremes*, p. 221.

64. Ibid., p. 497; cf. *The Age of Revolution*, p. 245.

65. Anderson, 'Darkness falls'.

66. *Age of Extremes*, pp. 10–11.

67. See Simon Bromley, 'The Long Twentieth Century', *Radical
    Philosophy*, 77, 1996.

68. Thus, '[j]ust how and why capitalism after the Second World
    War found itself ... surging forward ... is perhaps the major
    question which faces historians of the twentieth century.
    There is as yet no agreement on an answer, nor can I claim
    to provide a persuasive one': *Age of Extremes*, p. 8. For the
    absence of a 'persuasive explanation' of the onset of crisis
    in the 1970s, see ibid., p. 404.

69. Ibid., p. 270.

70. Ibid., p. 8.

71. Ibid., p. 9.

72. See W.W. Rostow, *The Stages of Economic Growth:
    A Non-Communist Manifesto*, 3rd edition, Cambridge:
    Cambridge University Press, 1990, pp. 162–4. In *Interesting
    Times* (p. 390), Hobsbawm, not altogether inaccurately,
    renders Rostow's sub-title 'An Anti-Communist Manifesto'.

73. *Age of Extremes*, p. 498.

74. See Gareth Stedman Jones, 'Marx's *Critique of Political
    Economy*: A Theory of History or a Theory of Communism?',
    in Wickham (ed.), *Marxist History-writing for the
    Twenty-first Century*, p. 150.

75. *Interesting Times*, pp. 127, 56. In the Preface to the US
    Paperback Edition (p. xiii), Hobsbawm writes that 'it was
    probably destined to fail' – an adverbial distinction with a
    substantial difference.

76. See Eric Hobsbawm, 'Can We Write the History of the Russian
    Revolution?' (1996), reprinted in *On History*, pp. 326–7.
    'The failure of revolution elsewhere', Hobsbawm wrote in
    Age of Extremes (pp. 497–8), 'left the USSR committed to
    build socialism alone, in a country in which, by the universal
    consensus of Marxists in 1917 ... the conditions for so doing
    were simply not present. The attempt to do so produced
    remarkable achievements – not least the ability to defeat

Germany in the Second War – but at a quite enormous and intolerable human cost, and at the cost of what proved to be a dead-end economy and a political system for which there was nothing to be said.'

77. *Age of Extremes*, p. 84.
78. 'Can We Write the History of the Russian Revolution?', p. 333. See also 'Goodbye to All That', pp. 122–3.
79. 'Goodbye to All That', p. 122.
80. *Age of Extremes*, p. 7.
81. Francis Mulhern, private communication; *Age of Extremes*, p. 112. See also p. 145, where Hobsbawm refers to Hitler's commitment to 'the destruction of the values and institutions of the "Western civilization" of the Age of Revolution'. As Neal Ascherson has remarked, Hobsbawm is 'the last British historian to use the word "civilisation" with complete confidence': 'The age of Hobsbawm', *Independent*, 2 October 1994.
82. *Age of Extremes*, p. 144. Consequently, it is 'an ex post facto rationalization which makes Lenin and Stalin the excuse for fascism' (p. 126). Hobsbawm was alluding to the argument developed by the German historian Ernst Nolte in the 1980s. For the French edition of his important book, see *La Guerre civile européenne 1917–1945. National-socialisme et bolchevisme*, trans. Jean-Marie Argelès, Paris: Syrtes, 2000.
83. See *Age of Extremes*, pp. 496–7.
84. See, e.g., ibid., pp. 411, 417, 424.
85. Ibid., p. 498. Cf. Eric Hobsbawm, 'Out of the Ashes' (1991), reprinted in Blackburn (ed.), *After the Fall*, especially pp. 323–5.
86. *Age of Extremes*, p. 563.
87. Ibid., p. 17.
88. Ibid., p. 16.
89. Ibid., p. 11.
90. Ibid., p. 15.
91. Ibid., p. 334. See also Eric Hobsbawm, 'Retreat of the male', *London Review of Books*, 4 August 2005.
92. *Age of Extremes*, p. 340.
93. Ibid., p. 421.
94. See, e.g., 'Out of the Ashes', p. 315.
95. *Age of Extremes*, pp. 446–7.
96. Ibid., p. 445.
97. Compare ibid., p. 298 with p. 447.

98. *Interesting Times*, p. 251.
99. Ibid., p. 83. Might Hobsbawm have had a part of himself in mind when, in *Age of Extremes* (p. 421), he alluded to 'public flaunting of the kind of behaviour which outraged the socially conventional or conservative ... who saw it as evidence of the breakdown of civilization, and darkly muttered "Weimar"'?
100. Eric Hobsbawm, 'The Sense of the Past' (1972), reprinted in *On History*, p. 25.
101. *Age of Extremes*, p. 565.
102. Ibid., p. 143.
103. Krzysztof Pomian, 'Quel xxe siecle?', *Le Débat*, 93, 1997, p. 42. Cf. Eric Hobsbawm, 'Commentaires', in ibid., pp. 85–8. For justification of the non-translation of *Age of Extremes* into French, see Pierre Nora, 'Traduire: necessité et difficultés', in ibid., pp. 93–5; and for its author's reflections on the fate of his book in the Hexagon, see *Interesting Times*, pp. 335–6.
104. *Age of Extremes*, pp. 558–9.
105. 'We ... lived under the black cloud of nuclear apocalypse': *Interesting Times*, p. 228.
106. *Age of Extremes*, p. 83.
107. Ibid., p. 251; 'Goodbye to All That', p. 115.
108. *Age of Extremes*, p. 168.
109. See ibid., p. 234: 'Like the USSR, the USA was a power representing an ideology, which most Americans believed to be a model for the world. Unlike the USSR, the USA was a democracy. Unfortunately it must be said that the second of these was probably the more dangerous.'
110. Ibid., p. 236.
111. Ibid., p. 56. In 'Barbarism: A User's Guide' (p. 346), Hobsbawm had offered another analogy when referring to 'the lunacies of the Cold War': 'a period which will one day be as hard to understand for historians as the witchcraze of the fifteenth and sixteenth centuries'.
112. *Age of Extremes*, pp. 249–50. See also ibid., p. 479 and *Interesting Times*, pp. 279–80.
113. *Interesting Times*, p. 279.
114. Eric Hobsbawm, 'The Centre Cannot Hold', *Marxism Today*, September 1991, p. 3; and see *Age of Extremes*, p. 483. In *The New Century* (p. 74) Hobsbawm was to write: 'If you compare the positive effects of the collapse of the Soviet Union and its political system with the negative ones, I would

say that the latter are undoubtedly greater. ... The scale of the human catastrophe that has struck Russia is something we simply don't understand in the West.'

115. *Age of Extremes*, p. 491.

116. See Eric Hobsbawm, 'The Crisis of Today's Ideologies', *New Left Review*, I/192, 1992, pp. 58–9. See also Preface to the US Paperback Edition, *Interesting Times*, p. xiv.

117. Michael Mann, 'As the Twentieth Century Ages', *New Left Review*, I/214, 1995, p. 112.

118. Polanyi, whom we have already encountered in Hobsbawm's work, is cited positively in *Age of Extremes*, pp. 342–3. For his diagnosis of the 'stark utopia' of a self-regulating market, conducive to nothing less than 'the demolition of society', see *Origins of Our Time: The Great Transformation*, London: Victor Gollancz, 1945, especially pp. 73–82. For Schumpeter, see *Capitalism, Socialism and Democracy*, London: Routledge, 1994, p. 139: 'In breaking down the pre-capitalist framework of society, capitalism ... broke not only barriers that impeded its progress, but also flying buttresses that prevented its collapse.' See also p. 162.

119. 'Commentaires', p. 90.

120. In 'Historians and Economists' (1980), reprinted in *On History*, Hobsbawm remarked that Schumpeter 'places both the forces that drive the system – the innovations which drive it forward, the sociological effects which bring it to an end – outside the system' (p. 142).

121. Justin Rosenberg, 'Hobsbawm's Century', *Monthly Review*, 47, 3, 1995, pp. 11–12.

122. Eric Hobsbawm, *Industry and Empire: From 1750 to the Present Day* (1968), Harmondsworth: Penguin, 1983, p. 225: 'The characteristic attitude of British or other governments towards the economy before the Industrial Revolution was that they had a duty to do something about it. This is the almost universal attitude of governments towards the economy today. But between these two eras, which represent what might be called the norm of history, and indeed of reason, there occurred an age in which the fundamental attitude of the government and the economists was the opposite. ... The history of government economic policy and theory since the Industrial Revolution is essentially that of the rise and fall of *laissez-faire*.' By the time of a new edition of the book in 1999, Hobsbawm had been obliged

significantly to revise this passage. In addition to replacing 'reason' by 'common sense', the final sentence now reads: 'the history of government economic policy and theory since the Industrial Revolution is essentially that of the rise, fall and revival of *laissez-faire*' (*Industry and Empire*, London: Penguin, 1999, p. 204).

123. *Age of Extremes*, p. 103.
124. Ibid., pp. 10, 176.
125. Ibid., pp. 409–10.
126. Ibid., p. 548.
127. Ibid., p. 412.
128. Ibid., pp. 563–4.
129. Ibid., p. 574.
130. Polanyi, *Origins of Our Time*, p. 145.
131. See Eric Hobsbawm, 'The Death of Neo-Liberalism', *Marxism Today*, November/December 1998; and see also *The New Century*, p. 71: 'The global crisis of 1997–98 may very well be taken as the turning-point.'
132. See *Interesting Times*, p. 279: 'Perhaps the bursting of the great speculative bubbles of the *fin-de-siècle*, 1997–2001, has finally broken the spell of market fundamentalism. The end of the hegemony of global neo-liberalism has been predicted and indeed announced long enough – I have done so myself more than once.'
133. *Age of Extremes*, p. 307.
134. See *Interesting Times*, p. 137; *Age of Extremes*, p. 388.
135. *Age of Extremes*, pp. 577–8.
136. Ibid., p. 579.
137. '[G]etting elected and then re-elected ... implies enormous quantities of lying in all its forms': Eric Hobsbawm, 'Identity Politics and the Left', *New Left Review*, I/217, 1996, p. 46. For André Tosel's coinage, see his *Un monde en abîme. Essai sur la mondialisation capitaliste*, Paris: Editions Kimé, 2008, p. 287.
138. See 'Identity Politics and the Left', p. 45. In *Interesting Times* (p. 416), Hobsbawm points to some of the biographical sources of his own ability 'to resist what Pascal called "the reasons of the heart of which reason knows nothing", namely emotional identification with some obvious or chosen group'.
139. Eric Hobsbawm, Preface to *Globalisation, Democracy and Terrorism*, p. 5. Adopting his by now customary posture, Hobsbawm signalled 'a small contribution to the necessary

task of cooling hot air through the application of reason and common sense'.

140. See Anderson, 'The Vanquished Left', p. 309. Cf. Luciano Canfora's splendid polemical history, *Democrazia. Storia di un' ideologia*, Rome and Bari: Laterza, 2004.

141. Chris Harman, 'The 20th Century: An Age of Extremes or An Age of Possibilities?', *International Socialism*, 85, 1999, p. 91. 'For Hobsbawm,' Harman noted (p. 92), 'the class-in-itself rarely makes its presence felt; the class-for-itself, never.'

142. See Mann, 'As the Twentieth Century Ages', p. 105.

143. See *Age of Extremes*, pp. 310–19; *The New Century*, p. 136.

144. Eric Hobsbawm, 'Notes on Class Consciousness' (1971), reprinted in *Worlds of Labour: Further Studies in the History of Labour*, London: Weidenfeld and Nicolson, 1984, p. 24.

145. Anderson, 'The Vanquished Left', p. 306.

146. Ibid., p. 305.

147. *Age of Extremes*, p. 580; and see also *Interesting Times*, p. 406.

148. See, e.g., *Age of Extremes*, pp. 241, 285.

149. Citing Anderson's criticism, a decade later Hobsbawm told an interviewer that 'if I had to do a major critique of my [trilogy], it would certainly be that I underplayed the U.S. ... I didn't see it as the up-and-coming power': 'Eric Hobsbawm's Interesting Times: An Interview with David Howell', *Socialist History*, 24, 2003, p. 13.

150. *Age of Extremes*, pp. 362, 405, 412–13.

151. Ibid., pp. 466, 467, 469, 470.

152. Ibid., p. 14.

153. *The Age of Empire*, p. 340.

154. *Age of Extremes*, p. 557.

155. *The New Century*, p. 162.

156. *Interesting Times*, p. xvi; and see also p. 6.

157. *The New Century*, p. 86 (my emphasis): 'We should not forget that, whatever yardstick is used, the majority of peoples are better off at the end of the twentieth century, in spite of the extraordinary catastrophes that have marked it. There are one or two exceptions, in which the situation has deteriorated, particularly in recent years in Africa and Russia. But overall, we have today three times the population there was at the start of the twentieth century, and all these people are physically stronger, taller, longer-living, and healthier. They suffer less hunger and famine, enjoy a

higher income, and have an immeasurably greater access to goods and services, including those which guarantee greater opportunities in life, such as education. This is also true of poorer countries' (p. 85).

158. *Age of Extremes*, p. 563.
159. Ibid., p. 559.
160. *The New Century*, p. 49.
161. *Interesting Times*, p. 412. Alluding to western support for Afghani jihadists in the 1980s, Hobsbawm had earlier legitimately reflected: '[t]he world may yet regret that, faced with Rosa Luxemburg's alternative of socialism or barbarism, it decided against socialism' (p. 281).
162. See Preface to *Globalisation, Democracy and Terrorism*, pp. 7 ff. As early as 1969, incidentally, Hobsbawm had noted an 'extraordinary devaluation ... of the word "genocide" in politics': 'The Rules of Violence', reprinted in *Revolutionaries*, p. 210.
163. Eric Hobsbawm, 'War, Peace and Hegemony at the Beginning of the Twenty-First Century' (2004), in *Globalisation, Democracy and Terrorism*, p. 46.
164. See ibid., p. 48; and see also Eric Hobsbawm, 'Terror', in *Globalisation, Democracy and Terrorism*, p. 137, where Hobsbawm maintains that 'the dangers of the "war against terror" do not come from Muslim suicide bombers'.
165. Ibid., pp. 128–9.
166. Eric Hobsbawm, 'Why American Hegemony Differs from the British Empire' (2005), in *Globalisation, Democracy and Terrorism*, pp. 70–1.
167. 'Terror', p. 137.
168. Eric Hobsbawm, 'The Empire Expands Wider Still and Wider' (2003), reprinted in *Globalisation, Democracy and Terrorism*, p. 161; see also 'War, Peace and Hegemony at the Beginning of the Twenty-First Century', p. 47.
169. See 'The Empire Expands Wider Still and Wider', p. 164.
170. See *Globalisation, Democracy and Terrorism*, pp. 47, 162, 163.
171. See, e.g., *Age of Extremes*, pp. 118, 127, 349, 567.
172. Ellen Meiksins Wood, *Empire of Capital*, London and New York: Verso, 2003, p. x.
173. Thus, in *Interesting Times* (p. 388), Roosevelt's presidency is bizarrely characterised as 'a government for the poor and the unions'. Even more implausibly, in *The New Century*

(p. 107), Hobsbawm writes of Clinton: 'the very fact that Clinton speaks in a certain manner means that by instinct he identifies with the values of the traditional Left. ... when Clinton won the presidency he looked like a Democrat in the best traditions of the American Left'.

174. Tosel, *Un monde en abîme*, p. 24.
175. *The New Century*, p. 58.
176. *Interesting Times*, p. 414.
177. Compare *Age of Extremes* p. 498 with p. 563.
178. *The New Century*, p. 102.
179. Ibid., p. 100. For two histories of the European left – one carrying an endorsement from Hobsbawm, the other by a pupil of his – see Geoff Eley, *Forging Democracy: The History of the Left in Europe, 1850–2000*, New York: Oxford University Press, 2002, and Donald Sassoon, *One Hundred Years of Socialism: The West European Left in the Twentieth Century*, London: I. B. Tauris, 1996.
180. See 'Out of the Ashes', pp. 323–5.
181. See *The New Century*, pp. 106, 107, 110; and see also *Interesting Times*, p. 277. Cf. Polanyi, *Origins of Our Time*, p. 77: 'A market economy can only exist in a market society.'
182. *Interesting Times*, p. 418.
183. Eric Hobsbawm, Introduction to Karl Marx and Frederick Engels, *The Communist Manifesto: A Modern Edition*, London and New York: Verso, p. 18.
184. Ibid., p. 22.
185. For a characteristically lucid brief discussion, rendered poignant by its author's imminent death, see G. A. Cohen, *Why Not Socialism?*, Princeton: Princeton University Press, 2009. Cf. Gregory Elliott, 'The Sorcerer and the Gravedigger: Karl Marx', in *Ends in Sight*.
186. Introduction to *The Communist Manifesto*, pp. 28–9.
187. Anderson, 'The Vanquished Left', p. 316.

Conclusion

1. Eric Hobsbawm, *Age of Extremes: The Short Twentieth Century, 1914–1991*, London: Michael Joseph, 1994, p. 87. See also *The Age of Empire 1875–1914* (1987), London: Weidenfeld and Nicolson, 1995, p. 334.
2. Eric Hobsbawm, interview with Edward Stourton, 'Today', BBC Radio 4, 18 October 2008.

3. Cf. Eric Hobsbawm, 'Intellectuals and the Class Struggle' (1971), reprinted in *Revolutionaries: Contemporary Essays* (1973), London: Phoenix, 1994, p. 256, n. 7: 'A friend, asked by his students, what the political consequences of the great slump of 1929 had been, answered: "First Hitler came to power. Then we lost the war in Spain. Finally we got the second world war and Hitler ruled most of Europe."'

4. Eric Hobsbawm, 'Socialism has failed. Now capitalism is bankrupt. So what comes next?', *Guardian*, 10 April 2009. The choice of title is unlikely to have been Hobsbawm's, though it would presumably have been cleared with so prestigious a contributor.

5. For a useful guide, see Andrew Gamble, *The Spectre at the Feast: Capitalist Crisis and the Politics of Recession*, Basingstoke: Palgrave Macmillan, 2009, Chapter 6.

6. See 'Eric Hobsbawm's Interesting Times: An Interview with David Howell', *Socialist History*, 24, 2003, p. 14.

7. Eric Hobsbawm, *Interesting Times: A Twentieth-Century Life* (2002), New York: The New Press, 2005, p. 277.

8. *Age of Extremes*, p. 103.

9. See Eric Hobsbawm, 'Marxist Historiography Today', in Chris Wickham (ed.), *Marxist History-writing for the Twenty-first Century*, Oxford: British Academy/Oxford University Press, 2007, pp. 183–5.

10. See Eric Hobsbawm, 'Marx and History' (1983/1984), reprinted in *On History* (1997), London: Abacus, 1998, p. 221.

11. 'Marxist Historiography Today', p. 187.

12. Eric Hobsbawm, Preface to the US Paperback Edition, *Interesting Times*, p. xii.

13. *Interesting Times*, p. 122.

14. Eric Hobsbawm, 'Address at the Funeral of Margot Heinemann 19 June 1992', in David Margolies and Maroula Joannou (eds), *Heart of the Heartless World: Essays in Cultural Resistance in Memory of Margot Heinemann*, London and Boulder (Colorado): Pluto Press, 1995, p. 217.

15. Ibid., p. 219.

BIBLIOGRAPHY

I. Writings by Eric Hobsbawm

Note: Only titles directly referred to in the main text or notes have been included here, listed in approximate chronological order. Where appropriate, the original date of publication has been given in square brackets, followed by full details of the actual edition used. Pending publication of a fully updated version, Keith McLelland's 1982 bibliography of Hobsbawm's writings (referenced below) remains indispensable.

(a) Books

(Ed.) *Labour's Turning Point 1880–1900* [1948], 2nd edition, Hassocks: Harvester Press, 1974.

Primitive Rebels: Studies in Archaic Forms of Social Movement in the 19th and 20th Centuries [1959], 3rd edition, Manchester: Manchester University Press, 1971.

(Originally as Francis Newton) *The Jazz Scene* [1959], revised edition, London: Weidenfeld and Nicolson, 1989.

The Age of Revolution: Europe 1789–1848 [1962], London: Weidenfeld and Nicolson, 1995.

Labouring Men: Studies in the History of Labour [1964], London: Weidenfeld and Nicolson, 1976.

(Ed.) Karl Marx, *Pre-Capitalist Economic Formations*, trans. Jack Cohen, London: Lawrence and Wishart, 1964.

Industry and Empire: From 1750 to the Present Day [1968], 2nd revised edition (with Chris Wrigley), London: Penguin, 1999.

(Co-author with George Rudé) *Captain Swing* [1968], Harmondsworth: Peregrine, 1985.

Bandits [1969], 2nd edition, Harmondsworth: Pelican, 1985.

Revolutionaries: Contemporary Essays [1973], London: Phoenix, 1994.

The Age of Capital 1848–1875 [1975], London: Weidenfeld and Nicolson, 1995.

The Italian Road to Socialism: An Interview by Eric Hobsbawm with Giorgio Napolitano of the Italian Communist Party, trans. John Cammett and Victoria DeGrazia, Westport, Connecticut and London: Lawrence Hill and Company/Journeyman Press, 1977.

(Co-editor with Georges Haupt et al.) *Storia del marxismo*, 4 vols in 5 parts, Turin: Einaudi, 1978–82. [Vol. 1 translated as *Marxism in Marx's Day*, Brighton: Harvester Press, 1982]

(Co-author with Ken Gill et al.) *The Forward March of Labour Halted?*, eds Martin Jacques and Francis Mulhern, London: Verso/*Marxism Today*, 1981.

Worlds of Labour: Further Studies in the History of Labour, London: Weidenfeld and Nicolson, 1984.

The Age of Empire 1875–1914 [1987], London: Weidenfeld and Nicolson, 1995.

Politics for a Rational Left: Political Writing 1977–1988, London and New York: Verso/*Marxism Today*, 1989.

Nations and Nationalism since 1780: Programme, Myth, Reality [1990], Canto edition, Cambridge: Cambridge University Press, 1991.

Echoes of the Marseillaise: Two Centuries Look Back on the French Revolution, London and New York: Verso, 1990.

Age of Extremes: The Short Twentieth Century, 1914–1991, London: Michael Joseph, 1994.

On History [1997], London: Abacus, 1998.

Uncommon People: Resistance, Rebellion and Jazz, London: Weidenfeld and Nicolson, 1998.

The New Century: Eric Hobsbawm in Conversation with Antonio Polito (1999), trans. Allan Cameron, London: Little, Brown, 2000.

Interesting Times: A Twentieth-Century Life [2002], New York: The New Press, 2005.

Globalisation, Democracy and Terrorism, London: Little, Brown, 2007.

(b) Other Texts

(With Raymond Williams) *War on the USSR?*, London: University Labour Federation, 1940.

'Drang nach Osten: some notes on German revisionism', *New Central European Observer*, 14 May 1949.

'Unrepentant apologetic' (review of Hjalmar Schacht, *Account Settled*), *New Central European Observer*, 4 May 1950.

Introduction to József Révai, *Lukács and Socialist Realism: A Hungarian Literary Controversy*, London: Fore Publications, 1950.

'The Taming of Parliamentary Democracy in Britain', *The Modern Quarterly*, new series, VI, 4, 1951.

(Co-author) 'Introduction', *Past and Present*, 1, 1952.

'Eric Hobsbawm's Communist Party Autobiography' [1952], *Socialist History*, 24, 2003.

'In Defence of the Thirties', *Granta*, 15 November 1952.

'The Crisis of the Seventeenth Century', *Past and Present*, 5 and 6, 1954; reprinted with a Postscript in Trevor Aston (ed.), *Crisis in Europe 1560–1660: Essays from 'Past and Present'*, London: Routledge and Kegan Paul, 1975.

'The British Communist Party', *Political Quarterly*, XXV, 1, 1954.

'Where are British Historians Going?', *Marxist Quarterly*, II, 1, 1955.

Letter to *Daily Worker*, 9 November 1956.

(Co-author) Letter to *New Statesman*, 1 December 1956.

'The Future of Marxism in the Social Sciences', *Universities and Left Review*, 1, 1957.

'Cuban prospects', *New Statesman*, 22 October 1960.

'Parliamentary Cretinism?' (review of Ralph Miliband, *Parliamentary Socialism*), *New Left Review*, I/12, 1961.

'Progress in History', *Marxism Today*, February 1962.

'From Feudalism to Capitalism', *Marxism Today*, September 1962; reprinted in Rodney Hilton et al., *The Transition from Feudalism to Capitalism*, London: New Left Books, 1976.

(As Francis Newton) 'Beatles and before', *New Statesman*, 8 November 1963.

'Organised orphans' (review of E. P. Thompson, *The Making of the English Working Class*), *New Statesman*, 29 November 1963.

(As Francis Newton) 'Bob Dylan', *New Statesman*, 22 May 1964.

'Maurice Dobb', in C. H. Feinstein (ed.), *Socialism, Capitalism and Economic Growth: Essays Presented to Maurice Dobb*, Cambridge: Cambridge University Press, 1967.

'The cultural congress of Havana', *Times Literary Supplement*, 25 January 1968.

'A hard man' (review of Che Guevara, *Reminiscences of the Cuban Revolutionary War*), *New Society*, 4 April 1968.

'Theory turned sideways', *Black Dwarf*, 1 June 1968.

'A special supplement: Chile: year one', *New York Review of Books*, 23 September 1971.

'The murder of Chile', *New Society*, 20 September 1973.

'The great Gramsci' (review of *Selections from the Prison Notebooks* and *Letters from Prison*), *New York Review of Books*, 4 April 1974.

'From Babylon to Manchester' (review of Perry Anderson, *Passages from Antiquity to Feudalism* and *Lineages of the Absolutist State*), *New Statesman*, 7 February 1975.

The Crisis and the Outlook, London: Birkbeck College Socialist Society, 1975.

'Look left' (review of Perry Anderson, *Considerations on Western Marxism*), *New Statesman*, 24 September 1976.

'Gramsci and Political Theory', *Marxism Today*, July 1977.

'1968 – A Retrospect', *Marxism Today*, May 1978.

'The new dissent: intellectuals, society and the left', *New Society*, 23 November 1978.

'The Historians' Group of the Communist Party', in Maurice Cornforth (ed.), *Rebels and their Causes: Essays in Honour of A. L. Morton*, London: Lawrence and Wishart, 1978.

'An Interview with Eric Hobsbawm', conducted by Pat Thane and Liz Lunbeck, *Radical History Review*, 19, 1978–79; reprinted in Henry Abelove et al. (eds), *Visions of History*, Manchester: Manchester University Press, 1983.

'Points of departure' (review of G. A. Cohen, *Karl Marx's Theory of History: A Defence*), *New Statesman*, 2 February 1979.

'Cambridge spy story – or the politics of treason' (review of Andrew Boyle, *The Climate of Treason*), *New Society*, 8 November 1979.

'In search of people's history' (review of Raphael Samuel, *People's History and Socialist Theory*, etc.), *London Review of Books*, 19 March–1 April, 1981.

'The State of the Left in Western Europe', *Marxism Today*, October 1982.

(With Christopher Hill and R. H. Hilton) '*Past and Present*: Origins and Early Years', *Past and Present*, 100, 1983.

'The Face of Labour's Future: Eric Hobsbawm Interviews Neil Kinnock', *Marxism Today*, October 1984.

(With Christopher Hill et al.) 'Agendas for Radical History', *Radical History Review*, 36, 1986.

'1956' (interview with Gareth Stedman Jones on the thirtieth anniversary of 1956), *Marxism Today*, November 1986.

'Revolution', in Roy Porter and Mikulás Teich (eds), *Revolution in History*, Cambridge: Cambridge University Press, 1986.

'Splitting Image' (interview with Achille Ochetto on the PCI), *Marxism Today*, February 1990.

'Goodbye to All That', *Marxism Today*, October 1990; reprinted in Robin Blackburn (ed.), *After the Fall: The Failure of Communism and the Future of Socialism*, London and New York: Verso, 1991.

'Out of the Ashes', *Marxism Today*, April 1991; reprinted in Robin Blackburn (ed.), *After the Fall: The Failure of Communism and the Future of Socialism*, London and New York: Verso, 1991.

'The Centre Cannot Hold', *Marxism Today*, September 1991.

'The Crisis of Today's Ideologies', *New Left Review*, I/192, 1992.

Obituary of E. P. Thompson, *Independent*, 30 August 1993.

'Address at the Funeral of Margot Heinemann, 19 June 1992', in David Margolies and Maroula Joanna (eds), *Heart of the Heartless World: Essays in Cultural Resistance in Memory of Margot Heinemann*, London: Pluto Press, 1995.

'Identity Politics and the Left', *New Left Review*, I/217, 1996.

'History and Illusion' (review of François Furet, *Le Passé d'une illusion*), *New Left Review*, I/220, 1996.

'Commentaires', *Le Débat*, 93, 1997.

Introduction to Karl Marx and Frederick Engels, *The Communist Manifesto: A Modern Edition*, London and New York: Verso, 1998.

'The Death of Neo-Liberalism', *Marxism Today*, special issue, November/December 1998.

'Eric Hobsbawm's Interesting Times: An Interview with David Howell', *Socialist History*, 24, 2003.

Comment on Pierre Vilar, *Guardian*, 17 September 2003.

Preface to the US Paperback Edition, *Interesting Times*, New York and London: New Press, 2005.

'Retreat of the male' (review of Göran Therborn, *Between Sex and Power*), *London Review of Books*, 4 August 2005.

'Could it have been different?' (review of Michael Korda, *Journey to a Revolution*, etc.), *London Review of Books*, 16 November 2006.

'War of ideas', *Guardian*, 17 February 2007.

'Cadres' (review of Raphael Samuel, *The Lost World of British Communism*, etc.), *London Review of Books*, 26 April 2007.

'Marxist Historiography Today', in Chris Wickham (ed.), *Marxist History-writing for the Twenty-first Century*, Oxford: British Academy/Oxford University Press, 2007.

'Memories of Weimar', *London Review of Books*, 24 January 2008.
'*LRB* contributors react to events in Gaza', *London Review of Books*, 15 January 2009.
Obituary of V. G. Kiernan, *Guardian*, 18 February 2009.
'Socialism has failed. Now capitalism is bankrupt. So what comes next?', *Guardian*, 10 April 2009.
Obituary of John Saville, *Guardian*, 16 June, 2009.

II. Secondary References

Abse, Tobias, 'Italy: A New Agenda', in Perry Anderson and Patrick Camiller (eds), *Mapping the West European Left*, London and New York: Verso/*New Left Review*, 1994.
Agosti, Aldo, *Bandiere rosse. Un profilo storico dei comunismi europei*, Rome: Riuniti, 1999.
Anderson, Perry, *In the Tracks of Historical Materialism*, London: New Left Books, 1983.
— 'The Ends of History', in *A Zone of Engagement*, London and New York: Verso, 1992.
— 'Darkness falls', *Guardian*, 8 November 1994.
— 'Eric Hobsbawm: The Vanquished Left', in Anderson, *Spectrum: From Right to Left in the World of Ideas*, London and New York: Verso, 2005.
Annan, Noel, *Our Age: The Generation That Made Post-War Britain*, London: Fontana, 1991.
Aron, Raymond, *The Opium of the Intellectuals*, trans. Terence Kilmartin, London: Secker and Warburg, 1957.
Ascherson, Neal, 'The age of Hobsbawm', *Independent*, 2 October 1994.
Bromley, Simon, 'The Long Twentieth Century', *Radical Philosophy*, 77, 1996.
Burleigh, Michael, 'Globalisation, democracy and terrorism', *The Times*, 15 July 2007.
Callaghan, John, *Cold War, Crisis and Conflict: The Communist Party of Great Britain, 1951–68*, London: Lawrence and Wishart, 2003.
Callinicos, Alex, 'The Drama of Revolution and Reaction: Marxist History and the Twentieth Century', in Chris Wickham (ed.), *Marxist History-writing for the Twenty-first Century*, Oxford: British Academy/Oxford University Press, 2007.
Canfora, Luciano, *La Democrazia. Storia di un'ideologia*, Rome and Bari: Laterza, 2004.

Cannadine, David, 'The strange death of liberal Europe', *New Society*, 23 October 1987.

Carlin, Norah and Birchall Ian, 'Kinnock's Favourite Marxist: Eric Hobsbawm and the Working Class', *International Socialism*, 21, autumn 1983.

Carrillo, Santiago, *'Eurocommunism' and the State*, trans. Nan Green and A. M. Elliott, London: Lawrence and Wishart, 1977.

Claudin, Fernando, *Eurocommunism and Socialism*, trans. John Wakeham, London: New Left Books, 1978.

Cohen, G. A., *Why Not Socialism?*, Princeton: Princeton University Press, 2009.

Collini, Stefan, 'Interesting times', *Independent*, 14 September 2002.

Communist Party of Great Britain, *The British Road to Socialism*, London 1951.

— *The British Road to Socialism*, London 1978.

Dimitrov, Georgi, *For the Unity of the Working Class Against Fascism: Report to the 7th Congress of the Communist International – 1935*, London: Red Star Press, 1975.

Durgan, Andy, *The Spanish Civil War*, Basingstoke: Palgrave Macmillan, 2007.

Eley, Geoff, *Forging Democracy: The History of the Left in Europe, 1850–2000*, New York: Oxford University Press, 2002.

— *A Crooked Line: From Cultural History to the History of Society*, Ann Arbor: University of Michigan Press, 2005.

Elliott, Gregory, *Labourism and the English Genius: The Strange Death of Labour England?*, London and New York: Verso, 1993.

— *Ends in Sight: Marx/Fukuyama/Hobsbawm/Anderson*, London and Ann Arbor: Pluto Press, 2008.

Engels, Frederick, *Anti-Dühring: Herr Eugen Dühring's Revolution in Science*, trans. Emile Burns, Moscow: Progress Publishers, 1977.

Ferguson, Niall, 'What a swell party it was ... for him', *Sunday Telegraph*, 20 October 2002.

Fine, Ben et al., 'Class Politics: An Answer to its Critics', London, pamphlet 1984.

Fowkes, Ben, *Communism in Germany under the Weimar Republic*, London and Basingstoke: Macmillan, 1984.

Furet, François, *Le Passé d'une illusion. Essai sur l'idée communiste au xxe siècle*, Paris: Robert Laffont, 1995.

Gallego, Marisa, *Eric Hobsbawm y la historia crítica del siglo xx*, Madrid: Campo de Ideas, 2005.

Gamble, Andrew, *The Spectre at the Feast: Capitalist Crisis and the Politics of Recession*, Basingstoke: Palgrave Macmillan, 2009.

Glover, Stephen, 'Why do we honour those who loathe Britain?', *Mail Online*, 7 March 2009.

Hall, Stuart and Jacques, Martin (eds), *The Politics of Thatcherism*, London: Lawrence and Wishart/*Marxism Today*, 1983.

— *New Times: The Changing Face of Politics in the 1990s*, London: Lawrence and Wishart/*Marxism Today*, 1989.

Harman, Chris, 'The 20th Century: An Age of Extremes or an Age of Possibilities?', *International Socialism*, 85, 1999.

Hill, Christopher, *Two Commonwealths*, London: George Harrup and co., 1945.

— *The English Revolution 1640: An Essay*, London: Lawrence and Wishart, 1979.

Jacques, Martin and Mulhern, Francis (eds), *The Forward March of Labour Halted?*, London: Verso/*Marxism Today*, 1981.

Jameson, Fredric, *Postmodernism, or The Cultural Logic of Late Capitalism*, London: Verso, 1991.

Judt, Tony, 'Downhill all the way', *New York Review of Books*, 25 May 1995.

— 'Eric Hobsbawm and the Romance of Communism', in *Reappraisals: Reflections on the Forgotten Twentieth Century*, London: Heinemann, 2008.

Kaye, Harvey J., *The British Marxist Historians: An Introductory Analysis*, revised edition, Basingstoke: Macmillan, 1995.

— *The Education of Desire: Marxism and the Writing of History*, New York and London: Routledge, 1993.

Kettle, Martin, 'MI5 cold-shoulders Hobsbawm request to see his file', *Guardian*, 2 March 2009.

Kiernan, V. G., 'Revolution and Reaction, 1789–1848', *New Left Review*, I/19, 1963.

— 'Victor Kiernan on Treason', in Jane Hindle (ed.), *London Review of Books: An Anthology*, London and New York: Verso, 1996.

Landes, David S., 'The ubiquitous bourgeoisie', *Times Literary Supplement*, 4 June 1976.

Levy, Geoffrey, 'Eric Hobsbawm, useful idiot of the chattering classes', *Mail Online*, 3 March 2009.

Magri, Lucio, *Il Sarto d'Ulm. Una possibile storia del PCI*, Milan: Il Saggiatore, 2009.

Mann, Michael, 'As the Twentieth Century Ages', *New Left Review*, I/214, 1995.

Marx, Karl, *Grundrisse: Foundations of the Critique of Political Economy*, trans. Martin Nicolaus, Harmondsworth: Penguin/ *New Left Review*, 1977.

— *Surveys from Exile*, Harmondsworth: Penguin/*New Left Review*, 1977.

— and Engels, Frederick, *Collected Works*, Vol. 4, London: Lawrence and Wishart, 1975.

— *Collected Works*, Vol. 5, London: Lawrence and Wishart, 1976

— *Collected Works*, Vol. 6, London: Lawrence and Wishart, 1976.

— *Selected Works*, Vol. 1, Moscow: Progress Publishers, 1977.

Mayer, Arno J., *The Persistence of the Old Regime: Europe to the Great War*, New York: Pantheon Books, 1981.

McDermott, Kevin and Agnew, Jeremy, *The Comintern: A History of International Communism from Lenin to Stalin*, Basingstoke: Macmillan, 1996.

McLelland, Keith, 'Bibliography of the Writings of Eric Hobsbawm', in Raphael Samuel and Gareth Stedman Jones (eds), *Culture, Ideology and Politics: Essays for Eric Hobsbawm*, London: Routledge and Kegan Paul, 1982.

Miliband, Ralph, 'The New Revisionism', *New Left Review*, I/150, 1985.

Morgan, Kevin, *Harry Pollitt*, Manchester: Manchester University Press, 1993.

Nolte, Ernst, *La Guerre civile européenne 1917–1945. National-socialisme et bolchevisme*, trans. Jean-Marie Argelès, Paris: Syrtes, 2000.

Nora, Pierre, 'Traduire: nécessité et difficultés', *Le Débat*, 93, 1997.

Panitch, Leo and Leys, Colin, *The End of Parliamentary Socialism: From New Left to New Labour*, London and New York: Verso, 1997.

Parker, David, *Ideology, Absolutism and the English Revolution: Debates of the British Communist Historians, 1940–1956*, London: Lawrence and Wishart, 2008.

Polanyi, Karl, *Origins of Our Time: The Great Transformation*, London: Victor Gollancz, 1945.

Pomian, Krzysztof, 'Quel xxe siècle', *Le Débat*, 93, January/ February 1993.

Poulantzas, Nicos, *State, Power, Socialism*, trans. Patrick Camiller, London: New Left Books, 1978.

Pryce-Jones, David, 'Eric Hobsbawm: Lying to the Credulous', *The New Criterion*, 21, 5, 2003.

Rosenberg, Justin, 'Hobsbawm's Century', *Monthly Review*, 47, 3, 1995.

Rostow, W.W., *The Stages of Economic Growth: A Non-Communist Manifesto*, third edition, Cambridge: Cambridge University Press, 1990.

Samuel, Raphael, 'British Marxist Historians, 1880–1980: Part One', *New Left Review*, I/120, 1980.

— and Stedman Jones, Gareth (eds), *Culture, Ideology and Politics: Essays for Eric Hobsbawm*, London: Routledge and Kegan Paul, 1982.

Sassoon, Donald, *One Hundred Years of Socialism: The West European Left in the Twentieth Century*, London: I. B. Tauris, 1996.

Saville, John (ed.), *Democracy and the Labour Movement: Essays in Honour of Dona Torr*, London: Lawrence and Wishart, 1954.

— 'The Twentieth Congress and the British Communist Party', *Socialist Register 1976*, London: Merlin Press, 1976.

— *Memoirs from the Left*, London: Merlin Press, 2002.

Schumpeter, Joseph, *Capitalism, Socialism and Democracy*, London: Routledge, 1994.

Schwarz, Bill, '"The People" in History: The Communist Party Historians' Group, 1946–1956', in Richard Johnson et al., *Making Histories: Studies in History-Writing and Politics*, London: Hutchinson, 1982.

Smith, Dai, *Raymond Williams: A Warrior's Tale*, Cardigan: Parthian, 2008.

Spriano, Paolo, *Stalin and the European Communists*, trans. Jon Rothschild, London: Verso, 1985.

Stedman Jones, Gareth, 'Society and Politics at the Beginning of the World Economy', *Cambridge Journal of Economics*, 1, 1977.

— 'Marx's *Critique of Political Economy*: A Theory of History or a Theory of Communism?', in Chris Wickham (ed.), *Marxist History-writing for the Twenty-first Century*, Oxford: British Academy/Oxford University Press, 2007.

Thane, Pat et al. (eds), *The Power of the Past: Essays for Eric Hobsbawm*, Cambridge and Paris: Cambridge University Press/ Editions de la Maison des Sciences de l'Homme, 1984.

Therborn, Göran, 'The Autobiography of the Twentieth Century', *New Left Review*, I/214, 1995.

Thompson, E. P., *The Poverty of Theory and Other Essays*, London: Merlin Press, 1978.

Thompson, Willie, *The Good Old Cause: British Communism 1920–1991*, London: Pluto Press, 1992.

Tosel, André, *Un monde en abîme. Essai sur la mondialisation capitaliste*, Paris: Editions Kimé, 2008.

Vilar, Pierre, *La Guerre d'Espagne*, Paris: Presses Universitaires de France, 1986.

Williams, Raymond, *Politics and Letters: Interviews with New Left Review*, London: New Left Books, 1979.

— *Loyalties*, London: Chatto and Windus, 1985.

Wood, Ellen Meiksins, *The Empire of Capital*, London and New York: Verso, 2003.

INDEX